THE GREAT
MODERN POETS

EDITED BY
MICHAEL SCHMIDT

Quercus

Contents

Introduction

In the twentieth century, poetry in English became more diverse and exciting than ever before. New varieties of English from America, the Caribbean, the Antipodes, India, North Africa and elsewhere, found their way into poetry, and new kinds of poetry were written. Traditional forms were sometimes reinvented; Modernism emerged with its insistent breaks with the immediate past, its different inventions, 'making it new' with elements from the distant past and from cultures remote in time and space. Poetry became a place of creative and critical conflict. A plethora of groups and movements emerged, defining themselves in opposition to one another or in relation to the past. Some – Imagism, for example – proved radical and important, marking a new point of departure for poetry; others were merely ephemeral, having more to do with marketing than with invention.

In any event, the old order changed, though at every stage a majority of writers and readers resisted the new and the alien. Modern poetry was seen as not rhyming, even when it did rhyme; as obscure and difficult, even when it was at its most lucid and limpid. The man or woman in the street, by the middle of the century, had rather a low opinion of the art, as though it had fallen on hard times in more ways than one. People 'knew what they liked', and it certainly wasn't that hard stuff they had been exposed to at school: Yeats and Eliot, Pound and Auden. They liked the sounds Dylan Thomas made, but what did it mean?

At the same time, because modern literature began being taught in school not long after the Second World War, specialist languages for describing modern poetry were evolving within academia. As strategies for reading and interpretation developed, poetry was incorporated into the syllabuses and, indeed, universities became one of the chief employers of poets.

Some poets still addressed a general reader, but at a level of not too taxing entertainment. The popular poem was generally short, memorable, either romantic or satirical. The long poem, the thought poem, the complex narrative and sustained satire, the elegy, the dramatic poem, were objects of study rather than of pleasure. Then poetry in performance began to revive what had been the popular readership for poetry. Poets would select for public recital poems which, in their view, an audience might grasp and enjoy. In due course, a performance poetry culture emerged, one in which what mattered was less the text on the page than its delivery, and the performer and audience became part of an almost collaborative process which might also entail music and dance. The successful performance poet could address enormous audiences on stage, through radio and television, and the book in such instances became little more than an inert programme or libretto, superfluous to the requirements of an audience and linguistically and aurally meagre on the page.

This anthology sets out to present some of the best poetry of the twentieth century, all of it written to be read, and to be read aloud, though not in the first instance to be performed. Each of the poets in this book intends the poem to be sounded. The reader who reads only for sense, rapidly running an eye across the lines without hearing the way the words work together, without getting the tongue, lips and teeth involved in the verse itself, will miss the poetry and probably the sense as well. This is because in poetry much of the sense and most of the pleasure reside in the sounds the poems make, the ways in which accented syllables balance with unaccented syllables; how the alliteration and assonance (the repetition and patterning of consonants, or of vowel sounds, within a line or over several lines) enact the sense, contribute to the tone; how the poem creates patterns of expectation through sound, and then plays variations, reversals, inversions. The reader does not need a technical vocabulary to read poetry (although a glossary is provided in this book to demystify some of the language commonly used when discussing poetry), only a voice in the head or out loud which can deliver the sounds. And in that delivery resides the crucial sense of the poem, a sense which entails pleasure.

The problem most readers have is that they want to understand through paraphrase. They want to compel the poem to make a prose statement. At school I was taught that poems have 'hidden meanings', which one could get at only by means of analysis, but once located the poem could be 'understood' and its magic in some way controlled. The opposite is true. Poems are wonderfully open, democratic spaces. They may ask us to read them several times before we understand the balances and contrasts, the lights and shadows, that they offer, but they are for the most part not deliberately obscure. Few make sense in the way prose makes sense. Those that seem to – Robert Frost's, for example, or William Carlos Williams's, or John Betjeman's – probably mean rather more than they seem to and they require more focused attention from us. No good poem makes common sense: the essence of a good poem is the uncommonness of the sense it makes. It is a structuring of words in which many meanings, or meanings at many levels, are enacted. If we read poems as prose, they have very little to say.

Prose and poetry are different in construction. You can lie back to read prose, and you can read it fast. You extract meaning from it: narrative, information and the like. You use it to tell things and it is generally an instrument of exposition and analysis, standing outside the things it names. Poetry, on the other hand, requires a different kind of attention and concentration. Not academic concentration, but rather a close attention to the actual language on the page, the words in this particular order, the stanzas in this particular shape, the rhymes falling where they fall, the effect they have on the ear and on the imagination. Prose uses the medium of language while poetry serves language and explores it.

Anyone who loves language, the ways in which a word carries its etymologies, for example, its history, and the ways in which in combination with other words those histories are elicited, is in serious danger of loving poetry. Those who love nursery rhyme and nonsense poetry are ideal readers of modern poetry. Not because modern poetry is nonsense – for that matter, nonsense poetry and nursery rhymes are themselves never nonsense either: think of the feelings they evoke, think of how they play the tongue and the heart. Such readers know that in poetry the sense is to be found in the sound as well as in the meanings of the words.

As for obscurities of reference, in Pound for example, and difficulties in argument or narrative, as in Yeats, Stevens and Auden, if the reader reads on and does not stop and puzzle and turn to reference books or Google, but finishes the poem, and then comes back and reads it again, in time (poetry being a language of accrual) the difficulties will resolve themselves. Eventually it may be useful to visit a dictionary or an atlas, but not until the sounds have lodged in the head. Often the context tells the reader as much as it is necessary to know.

I have tried to include some extracts from long poems and, in some cases, I represent a poet by a longish single poem. The short poem is everywhere privileged today: in magazines, newspapers, on radio, it is the column filler, the sound bite, the morsel. New readers who enjoy the ways in which language works will, in time, develop a hunger for sustained writing, perhaps the verse novels and epics of Les Murray and Derek Walcott, or the wonderful verse essays and sequences of Eliot, Pound and Auden.

Choosing 50 poets to represent a century was no easy matter. I have excluded most poets of my generation and the ones after on the grounds that their work belongs more to the twenty-first century than to the twentieth: it seemed wilful to confine them to an era which the millennium so decisively closed. Those that I have included are there because they made a substantial difference to the last decades of that century. More painful for me was the omission of poets whose work I love but who were too experimental for this kind of introductory volume, or who wrote only in extended forms and resisted excerpting, or who did things with language which others, represented here, did as well or better. The absence of these writers pains me because I would like to share and advocate their work in this context, but 50 is finite, and means the absence of Isaac Rosenberg, William Empson, Yvor Winters, Louis MacNeice, Hart Crane, Charles Olson, Louis Zukofsky, George Oppen and others of their generation, Randall Jarrell, Patrick Kavanagh, Austin Clarke, A.D. Hope, Judith Wright, Kenneth Koch, James Schuyler...

This anthology grows out of a conviction that readers can take a huge variety of pleasures from the poetry of a century in which the brutal acceleration of history, the revolutions in politics, technology, culture and society had an impact on this, the oldest verbal art known to mankind. In order to take these pleasures, certain prejudices have to be set aside and what C.H. Sisson calls a 'technique of ignorance' must be cultivated. In other words, you should approach these poems with no preconceptions and be open to the enjoyment they can bring.

The twentieth century is reflected if not recorded in the poetry included here. Poetry is, as Pound says, 'news that stays news' because new things happen, language is renewed, and that renewal remains renewing for each reader. Once the reader has set aside prejudices and prepared for pleasure and surprise, it is sensible to bear in mind that the best poems, whatever else they are, are unique. They are what with reference to Frank O'Hara's poems John Ashbery calls 'instances of themselves'. Larkin always insisted that we speak of poems rather than of poetry. It is an art of particulars, and each poem deserves separate saying and savouring.

FOR STELLA HALKYARD AND MARY GRIFFITHS

Thomas
Hardy
(1840–1928)

The Man He Killed

The Voice

The Convergence Of The Twain

In his own time Thomas Hardy was better known as novelist rather than poet, though he abandoned fiction and dedicated the last three decades of his life – the first three of the twentieth century – to poetry. Poetry was his first love: novels were a way of making a living, poetry a way of making sense of 'life's little ironies', and its bigger ones.

Hardy was born in Bockhampton, Dorset, in the third year of Queen Victoria's reign. His father was a builder and a musician. His mother had ambitions for her son and he received the best education his family could afford. An apprentice ecclesiastical architect from 1856–61, he specialized in the Gothic revival and developed real competence as a draftsman. From 1862–67 he worked in London at an architect's office and was awarded prizes by the Royal Institute of British Architects. The earliest of the poems he was ultimately to collect in *Wessex Poems* (1898) were written at this time. In 1870, encouraged by a friend, he began a career as a novelist with *Desperate Remedies* (1871). The impact of prose fiction on his verse is clear: he is almost always a story-teller.

'My opinion is that a poet should express the emotion of all the ages and the thought of his own.' Hardy's opinions emerge from long practice in prose and verse. 'The whole secret of living style and the difference between it and dead style, lies in it not having too much style.' Language must correspond in register to subject matter and be appropriate to occasion: a rustic plot demands plain diction; a poem on the loss of the *Titanic* ('The Convergence Of The Twain') a more sophisticated language, suited to the subject. Hardy uses metre and form to create poetic tension: some poems – 'The Man He Killed', for example – state one thing ('quaint and curious war is') but the hesitant syntax, and metrical disruption contradict what the speaker seems to be saying. Hardy uses (and discovers) a wider range of rhymed and metrical forms than any other modern English poet. His *oeuvre* amounts to almost a thousand poems.

In 1874 he married Emma Gifford, the sister-in-law of a parson whose church in Cornwall he helped to 'improve'. They were happy for a time, but passion cooled. Endurance replaced love, and more than 35 years' unhappiness elapsed before Emma died. At her death she became the faded muse of his great elegies of 1912–13. His mind was flooded by recollections; he experienced remorse and wrote love poems not at the age of 30, when he was courting, or at 34, when happily married, but in 1912, at 72 – one of life's ironies. In 1914 Hardy married a much younger woman, Florence Dugdale, who had been his literary assistant.

Sixty years old at the turn of the century, Thomas Hardy is the first poet who belongs to the twentieth century: familiar with the work of Darwin and of Einstein, he is caught between a new scientific approach and old religious verities. He is, in Donald Davie's words, 'the most far-reaching influence, for good or ill ... in British poetry of the last fifty years'. And not only British. He 'has the effect of locking any poet whom he influences into a world of historical contingency, a world of specific places at specific times.' W.H. Auden admired his 'hawk's vision, his way of looking at life from a very great height ... To see the individual life related not only to the local social life of its time, but to the whole of human history.'

The Man He Killed

'Had he and I but met
    By some old ancient inn,
We should have sat us down to wet
    Right many a nipperkin!

'But ranged as infantry,
    And staring face to face,
I shot at him and he at me,
    And killed him in his place.

'I shot him dead because –
    Because he was my foe,
Just so: my foe of course he was;
    That's clear enough; although

'He thought he'd 'list perhaps,
    Off-hand like – just as I –
'Was out of work – had sold his traps –
    No other reason why.

'Yes; quaint and curious war is!
    You shoot a fellow down
You'd treat if met where any bar is,
    Or help to half-a-crown.'

> Yes; quaint and curious war is!

The Voice

Woman much missed, how you call to me, call to me,
Saying that now you are not as you were
When you had changed from the one who was all to me,
But as at first, when our day was fair.

Can it be you that I hear? Let me view you, then,
Standing as when I drew near to the town
Where you would wait for me: yes, as I knew you then,
Even to the original air-blue gown!

Or is it only the breeze in its listlessness
Travelling across the wet mead to me here,
You being ever dissolved to wan wistlessness,
Heard no more again far or near?

    Thus I; faltering forward,
    Leaves around me falling,
Wind oozing thin through the thorn from norward,
    And the woman calling.

The Convergence Of The Twain

(Lines on the loss of the 'Titanic')

I   In a solitude of the sea
      Deep from human vanity,
And the Pride of Life that planned her, stilly couches she.

II   Steel chambers, late the pyres
      Of her salamandrine fires,
Cold currents thrid, and turn to rhythmic tidal lyres.

III   Over the mirrors meant
      To glass the opulent
The sea-worm crawls—grotesque, slimed, dumb, indifferent.

IV   Jewels in joy designed
      To ravish the sensuous mind
Lie lightless, all their sparkles bleared and black and blind.

V   Dim moon-eyed fishes near
      Gaze at the gilded gear
And query: 'What does this vaingloriousness down here?'...

VI   Well: while was fashioning
      This creature of cleaving wing,
The Immanent Will that stirs and urges everything

VII   Prepared a sinister mate
      For her — so gaily great—
A Shape of Ice, for the time far and dissociate.

VIII   And as the smart ship grew
      In stature, grace, and hue,
In shadowy silent distance grew the Iceberg too.

IX   Alien they seemed to be:
      No mortal eye could see
The intimate welding of their later history,

X   Or sign that they were bent
      By paths coincident
On being anon twin halves of one august event,

XI   Till the Spinner of the Years
      Said 'Now!' And each one hears,
And consummation comes, and jars two hemispheres.

Till the Spinner of the Years
Said 'Now!'

A.E. **Housman**

(1859–1936)

Reveille

Into my heart an air that kills …

Crossing alone the nighted ferry …

On Wenlock Edge the wood's in trouble …

From the day in 1896 when *A Shropshire Lad* was published until now, Alfred Edward Housman has been a best-selling poet. The poems are taken to heart and learned by heart, despite the austere character of the opinionated professor, the vindictive classical scholar, the repressed man who made them. The poems speak with an uncanny, classless refinement. They sing ageless themes of mortality, thwarted love and sacrifice.

Housman touches two poetic nerves: the one that responds to popular ballads, for his poems, in strategy, theme and tone often resemble elegiac ballads; and the one that responds to hymns, though his hymn stanzas celebrate no God. The poems are memorable. Phrases and stanzas come to mind at times of stress, or simply when one is out walking. Composers including George Butterworth in 1913 and Ralph Vaughan Williams in 1914 recognized song texts in the poems and set them to music.

A.E. Housman was born in Fockbury, Worcestershire. His background was conservative, middle-class, cultured and conducive to the development of the interest in literature that was to mature into a passion for classical studies. He enjoyed escaping into the countryside for walks and the eastern horizon of these youthful rambles was Shropshire.

Educated at Bromsgrove, Worcester, and then at Oxford, he became an outstanding textual critic, so involved in his texts that he omitted to revise ancient history and philosophy and failed to take even a pass degree. He entered a Civil Service job in the Patent Office. After 11 years there his classical achievements earned him a professorial chair in Latin at University College, London, where he worked for the next decade. There he published *A Shropshire Lad*. In 1911 he became Professor of Latin at Cambridge, a post he held until the end of his life. His editions of Manilius, Juvenal and Lucan are magisterial.

A Shropshire Lad achieved for him almost immediate fame as a poet. It was 26 years before he published another collection, called simply *Last Poems*. This was followed, as 'last poems' sometimes are, by *More Poems*, a collection issued in 1936. He died later in the same year. The *Collected Poems* is slim for a poet who lived to 77 – slim in several ways. There is little variation of theme and mood, the poems do not develop in terms of form and language and can seem to parody themselves. If, as biographers suggest, he came to terms, to some troubled extent, with his homosexuality, the poems touch on this only obliquely, unless we read them as encoded expressions of a private odyssey, in which case we displace the poetry with speculative biography.

Housman expressed his public attitude to poetry most fully in a lecture, 'The Name and Nature of Poetry', delivered in 1933. He condemned the 'difficult' poetry of the metaphysicals and by implication discredited the new poetry of the twentieth century. Poetry was for him not an intellectual but a physical experience. A poem's effect had to do with music, rhyme and emotional direction, not *meaning* as such.

We cannot conveniently label his verse: the forms are classical, the content romantic; the forms are simple, the content at times sophisticated; the forms are derivative, the content, masked as it sometimes must be, feels original. He is a classical poet and a classicist of accomplishment, for whom the classics are a source of imaginative life; but he has a romantic temperament. The world to which his romanticism is confined confronts him, as it does Hardy, with teeming paradoxes, inscrutable irony.

Reveille

Wake: the silver dusk returning
    Up the beach of darkness brims,
And the ship of sunrise burning
    Strands upon the eastern rims.

Wake: the vaulted shadow shatters,
    Trampled to the floor it spanned,
And the tent of night in tatters
    Straws the sky-pavilioned land.

Up, lad, up, 'tis late for lying:
    Hear the drums of morning play;
Hark, the empty highways crying
    'Who'll beyond the hills away?'

Towns and countries woo together,
    Forelands beacon, belfries call;
Never lad that trod on leather
    Lived to feast his heart with all.

Up, lad: thews that lie and cumber
    Sunlit pallets never thrive;
Morns abed and daylight slumber
    Were not meant for man alive.

Clay lies still, but blood's a rover;
    Breath's a ware that will not keep.
Up, lad: when the journey's over
    There'll be time enough to sleep.

Up, lad, up, 'tis
late for lying:
    Hear the
drums of
morning play

Into my heart an air that kills...

Into my heart an air that kills
    From yon far country blows:
What are those blue remembered hills,
    What spires, what farms are those?

That is the land of lost content,
    I see it shining plain,
The happy highways where I went
    And cannot come again.

Crossing alone the nighted ferry…

Crossing alone the nighted ferry
    With the one coin for fee,
Whom, on the wharf of Lethe waiting,
    Count you to find? Not me.

The brisk fond lackey to fetch and carry,
    The true, sick-hearted slave,
Expect him not in the just city
    And free land of the grave.

On Wenlock Edge the wood's in trouble…

On Wenlock Edge the wood's in trouble;
    His forest fleece the Wrekin heaves;
The gale, it plies the saplings double,
    And thick on Severn snow the leaves.

'Twould blow like this through holt and hanger
    When Uricon the city stood:
'Tis the old wind in the old anger,
    But then it threshed another wood.

Then, 'twas before my time, the Roman
    At yonder heaving hill would stare:
The blood that warms an English yeoman,
    The thoughts that hurt him, they were there.

There, like the wind through woods in riot,
    Through him the gale of life blew high;
The tree of man was never quiet:
    Then 'twas the Roman, now 'tis I.

The gale, it plies the saplings double,
    It blows so hard, 'twill soon be gone:
To-day the Roman and his trouble
    Are ashes under Uricon.

The tree of man was never quiet

Rudyard
Kipling
(1865–1936)

Mesopotamia 1917

The Storm Cone

My Boy Jack

Joseph Rudyard Kipling was born in Bombay. 'Rudyard' refers to Rudyard Lake in Staffordshire where his mother and father courted. His father was a teacher of sculpture at the Bombay School of Art and later curator of the museum at Lahore. His mother was the sister of Lady Burne-Jones and of Stanley Baldwin's mother – wives, respectively, of the most famous painter of the day, and of a Prime Minister. His backgrounds were intellectually lively, socially privileged, and yet shared in different and older cultures. India in his early years was real to him as something mysterious and compelling. His imaginative world began here, and his memory. As an infant he was under the care of an Indian nurse and learned Hindustani as well as English. When as a little sahib he went to England, he stood at an awkward angle to the Colonial world; the country he came to lacked warmth, colour and easy intimacy. When he returned to India as a young man, he had changed. He invests much energy in reclaiming the original India.

He was six when he arrived in England for his education, first to the home of an elderly evangelical relation in Southsea. His miserable six years there ('the House of Desolation') were relieved by visits to the Burne-Jones establishment near Brighton. There William Morris became Uncle Topsy. Sir Edward Burne-Jones was at work on illustrations for Morris's Kelmscott Press edition of Chaucer's *Canterbury Tales*. Apart from these rare outings, the boy endured a life of unhappiness, moving in 1879 to a minor public school, the United Services College, Westward Ho!, in Devon. There he began writing verse.

His first book, *Schoolboy Lyrics*, was privately printed in 1881. The next year, at 16, he returned to India and served on the staff of the Lahore *Civil and Military Gazette*. In 1889 he became foreign correspondent for the Allahabad *Pioneer* and began travelling – to China, Japan, America, Australia and Africa. As a correspondent he became a keen observer. He saw deeply into Indian – and not only Indian – affairs, with the perspective of one who understands his own British tribal priorities, but also the needs of a loved other world.

The light verse he wrote for newspapers was collected in *Departmental Ditties* (1886). But it was *Plain Tales from the Hills* (1888) that made a real mark in England and paved the way for his return. He arrived in London in 1889 with a reputation. This was the period of his greatest popularity – until 1902 he was the most eloquent literary spokesman for a Tory populism which was patriotic, imperial and *responsible*.

His first major success, *Barrack Room Ballads* (1892, 1896), contains many of his best-known poems. Hymns, music-hall songs, ballads and public poetry lay behind his instantly popular verse. Such was his reputation that, after Tennyson's death, he was offered the Poet Laureateship. He refused – this was the first of several honours he declined. He declined even the Order of Merit, and when he finally came to rest at Westminster Abbey, his name was 'unenhanced'.

Kipling married the American Caroline Balestier, lived for five not pleasant years on her family estate in Vermont, and in 1897 returned to England for good, settling first at The Elms, Rottingdean, Sussex, and then in 1902 acquiring Bateman's, Burwash, from which he stirred abroad only occasionally in the last 34 years of his life. He was still a relatively young man, but he had wearied of travel. During the First World War be became an elegist. The death of his own son informs 'My Boy Jack', a poem of generalized loss.

Mesopotamia 1917

They shall not return to us, the resolute, the young,
    The eager and whole-hearted whom we gave:
But the men who left them thriftily to die in their own dung,
    Shall they come with years and honour to the grave?

They shall not return to us, the strong men coldly slain
    In sight of help denied from day to day:
But the men who edged their agonies and chid them in their pain,
    Are they too strong and wise to put away?

Our dead shall not return to us while Day and Night divide —
    Never while the bars of sunset hold.
But the idle-minded overlings who quibbled while they died,
    Shall they thrust for high employments as of old?

Shall we only threaten and be angry for an hour?
    When the storm is ended shall we find
How softly but how swiftly they have sidled back to power
    By the favour and contrivance of their kind?

Even while they soothe us, while they promise large amends,
    Even while they make a show of fear,
Do they call upon their debtors, and take counsel with their friends,
    To confirm and re-establish each career?

Their lives cannot repay us — their death could not undo —
    The shame that they have laid upon our race.
But the slothfulness that wasted and the arrogance that slew,
    Shall we leave it unabated in its place?

The Storm Cone

This is the midnight — let no star
Delude us — dawn is very far.
This is the tempest long foretold—
Slow to make head but sure to hold.

Stand by! The lull 'twixt blast and blast
Signals the storm is near, not past;
And worse than present jeopardy
May our forlorn to-morrow be.

If we have cleared the expectant reef,
Let no man look for his relief.
Only the darkness hides the shape
Of further peril to escape.

It is decreed that we abide
The weight of gale against the tide
And those huge waves the outer main
Sends in to set us back again.

They fall and whelm. We strain to hear
The pulses of her labouring gear,
Till the deep throb beneath us proves,
After each shudder and check, she moves!

She moves, with all save purpose lost,
To make her offing from the coast;
But, till she fetches open sea,
Let no man deem that he is free!

Only the darkness hides the shape
Of further peril to escape.

My Boy Jack

'Have you news of my boy Jack?'
    Not this tide.
'When d'you think that he'll come back?'
Not with this wind blowing, and this tide.

'Has anyone else had word of him?'
    Not this tide.
For what is sunk will hardly swim,
Not with this wind blowing and this tide.

'Oh, dear, what comfort can I find?'
    None this tide,
    Nor any tide,
Except he did not shame his kind—
Not even with that wind blowing, and that tide.

Then hold your head up all the more,
    This tide,
    And every tide;
Because he was the son you bore,
And gave to that wind blowing and that tide!

W.B. **Yeats**

(1865–1939)

Yeats's life is a tangle of fortuitous meetings, chance influences and intellectual inconsistencies. Within his work he never stood still but built and built on what had come before. His more-than-half-a-century of verse constitutes an *oeuvre* at once exemplary and coherent but also curiously 'staged', deliberately heroic, in which the figures, closely observed, seem to be wearing stilts.

William Butler Yeats was born in Dublin. His father John was an original and accomplished painter. His mother Susan Pollexfen was of established Anglo-Irish extraction. Yeats liked to consider her aristocratic. The Anglo-Irish background – Protestant in religion, Republican in sentiment – was marked by strongly held and hotly debated opinions, not least on art and literature. Much of his childhood he spent in London, where his parents moved in 1867. They lived off income from family lands in Kildare until 1880 when the Land War put an end to it. In 1875 Yeats entered the Godolphin School in Hammersmith and visited Ireland during the longer school vacations, when he stayed with the Pollexfens in County Sligo. His poems began to be published in 1885. A year later he attended his first séance. A passion for spiritualism and magic was already far advanced: whatever voices he heard on that occasion further exacerbated his enthusiasm.

In 1908 his *Collected Works* appeared in eight volumes. He was 43, a poet of established reputation, a dramatist and prose writer, a lecturer at home and abroad. He had reached the end of his first period of creative activity. Critics lay insufficient stress on the rejuvenating effect Ezra Pound had on Yeats's development. Returning from the funeral of the playwright John Millington Synge in 1909, he met the young Pound. Pound had admired his work since he was a schoolboy. They became totally engrossed in composition and revision, and Pound's chief contribution was to make the Irish poet acutely aware of the force of transitive verbs, the positive effect of economy in the use of adjectives and adverbs, and the centrality of living rhythm and metre, not a mechanical following of the rules but an authoritative engagement with them.

He became a man much honoured, receiving the Nobel Prize for Literature in 1923 and later becoming a Senator in the Irish Parliament. In 1924, suffering from high blood pressure and respiratory problems, he went to Sicily for a change of climate. There he was enthralled by the Byzantine mosaics. In his illness he entered an intensely creative period, composing *The Tower* poems and some of *The Winding Stair*. His friends' deaths, his own slow physical deterioration, the political turmoil of Ireland and Europe, bore in upon him.

In 'Coole Park and Ballylee, 1931' he writes, 'We were the last romantics – chose for theme / Traditional sanctity and loveliness', embattled in a world hostile to art. 'My poetry is generally written out of despair', he reports. 'Like Balzac, I see increasing commonness everywhere, and like Balzac I know no one who shares the premises from which I work.'

From the outset he had two stylistic strains in his writing: a highly cadenced style for shadows and mystery; and a stark, phrased, declarative style, with precise images for specific meanings. His development is in the shifting balance between the two styles in response to changes in his ambitions and passions. The early poetry belongs in the nineteenth century, with its mellifluousness and twilight, its myth and helpless legend. The work of his second maturity, however, set a severe agenda for Irish poetry, and much that has followed has been an attempt to find new, or different, ground.

An Irish Airman Foresees His Death

I know that I shall meet my fate
Somewhere among the clouds above;
Those that I fight I do not hate,
Those that I guard I do not love;
My country is Kiltartan Cross,
My countrymen Kiltartan's poor,
No likely end could bring them loss
Or leave them happier than before.
Nor law, nor duty bade me fight,
Nor public men, nor cheering crowds,
A lonely impulse of delight
Drove to this tumult in the clouds;
I balanced all, brought all to mind,
The years to come seemed waste of breath,
A waste of breath the years behind
In balance with this life, this death.

A lonely impulse
of delight

Leda and the Swan

A sudden blow: the great wings beating still
Above the staggering girl, her thighs caressed
By the dark webs, her nape caught in his bill,
He holds her helpless breast upon his breast.

How can those terrified vague fingers push
The feathered glory from her loosening thighs?
And how can body, laid in that white rush,
But feel the strange heart beating where it lies?

A shudder in the loins engenders there
The broken wall, the burning roof and tower
And Agamemnon dead.
                              Being so caught up,
So mastered by the brute blood of the air,
Did she put on his knowledge with his power
Before the indifferent beak could let her drop?

Did she put on
his knowledge with his power

Easter 1916

I have met them at close of day
Coming with vivid faces
From counter or desk among grey
Eighteenth-century houses.
I have passed with a nod of the head
Or polite meaningless words,
Or have lingered awhile and said
Polite meaningless words,
And thought before I had done
Of a mocking tale or a gibe
To please a companion
Around the fire at the club,
Being certain that they and I
But lived where motley is worn:
All changed, changed utterly:
A terrible beauty is born.

That woman's days were spent
In ignorant good-will,
Her nights in argument
Until her voice grew shrill.
What voice more sweet than hers
When, young and beautiful,
She rode to harriers?
This man had kept a school
And rode our wingèd horse;
This other his helper and friend
Was coming into his force;
He might have won fame in the end,
So sensitive his nature seemed,
So daring and sweet his thought.
This other man I had dreamed
A drunken, vain glorious lout.
He had done most bitter wrong
To some who are near my heart,
Yet I number him in the song;
He, too, has resigned his part
In the casual comedy;
He, too, has been changed in his turn,
Transformed utterly:
A terrible beauty is born.

Hearts with one purpose alone
Through summer and winter seem
Enchanted to a stone
To trouble the living stream.
The horse that comes from the road,
The rider, the birds that range
From cloud to tumbling cloud,
Minute by minute they change;
A shadow of cloud on the stream
Changes minute by minute;
A horse-hoof slides on the brim,
And a horse plashes within it;
Where long-legged moor-hens dive,
And hens to moor-cocks call;
Minute by minute they live:
The stone's in the midst of all.

Too long a sacrifice
Can make a stone of the heart.
O when may it suffice?
That is Heaven's part, our part
To murmur name upon name,
As a mother names her child
When sleep at last has come
On limbs that had run wild.
What is it but nightfall?
No, no, not night but death;
Was it needless death after all?
For England may keep faith
For all that is done and said.
We know their dream; enough
To know they dreamed and are dead;
And what if excess of love
Bewildered them till they died?
I write it out in a verse —
MacDonagh and MacBride
And Connolly and Pearse
Now and in time to be,
Wherever green is worn,
Are changed, changed utterly:
A terrible beauty is born.

The Second Coming

Turning and turning in the widening gyre
The falcon cannot hear the falconer;
Things fall apart; the centre cannot hold;
Mere anarchy is loosed upon the world,
The blood-dimmed tide is loosed, and everywhere
The ceremony of innocence is drowned;
The best lack all conviction, while the worst
Are full of passionate intensity.

Surely some revelation is at hand;
Surely the Second Coming is at hand.
The Second Coming! Hardly are those words out
When a vast image out of *Spiritus Mundi*
Troubles my sight: somewhere in sands of the desert
A shape with lion body and the head of a man,
A gaze blank and pitiless as the sun,
Is moving its slow thighs, while all about it
Reel shadows of the indignant desert birds.
The darkness drops again; but now I know
That twenty centuries of stony sleep
Were vexed to nightmare by a rocking cradle,
And what rough beast, its hour come round at last,
Slouches towards Bethlehem to be born?

Things fall apart; the centre cannot hold

Sailing to Byzantium

I
That is no country for old men. The young
In one another's arms, birds in the trees
—Those dying generations — at their song,
The salmon-falls, the mackerel-crowded seas,
Fish, flesh, or fowl, commend all summer long
Whatever is begotten, born, and dies.
Caught in that sensual music all neglect
Monuments of unageing intellect.

II
An aged man is but a paltry thing,
A tattered coat upon a stick, unless
Soul clap its hands and sing, and louder sing
For every tatter in its mortal dress,
Nor is there singing school but studying
Monuments of its own magnificence;

and gather me
Into the artifice
of eternity

And therefore I have sailed the seas and come
To the holy city of Byzantium.

III
O sages standing in God's holy fire
As in the gold mosaic of a wall,
Come from the holy fire, perne in a gyre,
And be the singing-masters of my soul.
Consume my heart away; sick with desire
And fastened to a dying animal
It knows not what it is; and gather me
Into the artifice of eternity.

IV
Once out of nature I shall never take
My bodily form from any natural thing,
But such a form as Grecian goldsmiths make
Of hammered gold and gold enamelling
To keep a drowsy Emperor awake;
Or set upon a golden bough to sing
To lords and ladies of Byzantium
Of what is past, or passing, or to come.

Long-Legged Fly

That civilisation may not sink,
Its great battle lost,
Quiet the dog, tether the pony
To a distant post;
Our master Caesar is in the tent
Where the maps are spread,
His eyes fixed upon nothing,
A hand under his head.

*Like a long-legged fly upon the stream
His mind moves upon silence.*

That the topless towers be burnt
And men recall that face,
Move most gently if move you must
In this lonely place.
She thinks, part woman, three parts a child,
That nobody looks; her feet

Practise a tinker shuffle
Picked up on a street.

*Like a long-legged fly upon the stream
Her mind moves upon silence.*

That girls at puberty may find
The first Adam in their thought,
Shut the door of the Pope's chapel,
Keep those children out.
There on that scaffolding reclines
Michael Angelo.
With no more sound than the mice make
His hand moves to and fro.

*Like a long-legged fly upon the stream
His mind moves upon silence.*

Charlotte
Mew
(1869–1928)

Charlotte Mew was among Thomas Hardy's favourite female writers. Yet despite the burgeoning interest in early twentieth century women's writing, and even after a biography which anatomized her eccentricities and a novel that imagines a romantic dalliance with Hardy, her work has only lately been recognized for its radical originality. In 1953, before Sylvia Plath altered the map of English poetry, Mew was seen, if seen at all, as a pathetic figure. Her friend and champion Alida Monro's edition of her poems that year looked like an act of piety. Twenty years later readers might have been more ready for the poems, but in a chunky volume that included all of her stories they were lost under the weight of indifferent prose. Now, at last, her originality of form and theme, her electrifying uniqueness are finding her a readership.

Her life was neither easy nor happy. She was born in London into a moderately well-to-do family. Her father, an architect, had come to London and married his boss's daughter, who was one for keeping up appearances. When financial hardship beset the Mews, she insisted on maintaining a genteel front. When it became necessary to let out a room to lodgers, this was kept secret from all but the most intimate acquaintances, of which there were very few. Young Charlotte enjoyed the education of a Victorian lady, was taught no skills and never went – in formal education – beyond the Lucy Harrison School for Girls in Gower Street. She never mastered the rules of punctuation.

When her father died – she was 29 and still living at home – he left almost nothing. Charlotte, her sister Anne and their mother suffered to remain 'proper' and survive. Anne was an artist specializing in furniture restoration. Charlotte could teach. The anguish of earning their way became a permanent torment: they had not been reared to this. In the year of her suicide, Charlotte was awarded a Civil List Pension – but it came too late.

Charlotte's infrequent travels, to northern France especially, marked her imagination. When she reached the peak of her poetic powers between 1909–16, writing with confidence and urgency, she set several poems in France. She invented the very, very long line, and she varied line lengths and rhymes to great effect in her poems. Temperamentally an urban poet, of characters in cities, rooms and passageways, she evokes confined, gendered spaces. Even the poems set in the English countryside have an enclosing quality. She knew rural England as a visitor, seeing it through the eyes of poets she admired, notably Hardy.

Despite her reticence, she urgently needed to express something, the nature of which she herself did not completely grasp. Given the hardships she experienced, her emotional nature and her educational background, it is astonishing that – after the unpromising early prose romances – she did not create a fantastic, escapist world. Instead, she began to develop a style that engaged with her reality at its most vulnerable and exposed. Her two books, *The Farmer's Bride* (1916) and *The Rambling Sailor* (1929), which appeared posthumously, contain the core of her work.

'Things that kill us seem / Blind to the death they give,' she wrote in 'The Quiet House', a poem she reckoned her most subjective. In it the writing is as sharp and harrowing as that of Sylvia Plath: 'A rose can stab you across the street / Deeper than any knife: / And the crimson haunts you everywhere – / Thin shafts of sunlight, like the ghosts of reddened swords have struck our stair / As if, coming down, you had spilt your life.'

Fame

Sometimes in the over-heated house, but not for long,
    Smirking and speaking rather loud,
    I see myself among the crowd,
Where no one fits the singer to his song,
Or sifts the unpainted from the painted faces
Of the people who are always on my stair;
They were not with me when I walked in heavenly places;
        But could I spare
In the blind Earth's great silences and spaces,
    The din, the scuffle, the long stare
    If I went back and it was not there?
Back to the old known things that are the new,
The folded glory of the gorse, the sweet-briar air,
To the larks that cannot praise us, knowing nothing of what we do
    And the divine, wise trees that do not care
Yet, to leave Fame, still with such eyes and that bright hair!
God! If I might! And before I go hence
        Take in her stead
        To our tossed bed,
One little dream, no matter how small, how wild.
Just now, I think I found it in a field, under a fence –
A frail, dead, new-born lamb, ghostly and pitiful and white,
        A blot upon the night,
        The moon's dropped child!

> And the
> divine, wise
> trees that
> do not care

Not for that City

Not for that city of the level sun,
        Its golden streets and glittering gates ablaze –
        The shadeless, sleepless city of white days,
White nights, or nights and days that are as one –
We weary, when all is said, all thought, all done.
        We strain our eyes beyond the dusk to see
        What, from the threshold of eternity
We shall step into. No, I think we shun
The splendour of that everlasting glare,
        The clamour of that never-ending song.
        And if for anything we greatly long
It is for some remote and quiet stair
        Which winds to silence and a space for sleep
        Too sound for waking and for dreams too deep.

Sea Love

Tide be runnin' the great world over;
    T'was only last June-month, I mind, that we
Was thinkin' the toss and call in the breast of the lover
    So everlastin' as the sea.

Heer's the same little fishies that sputter and swim
    Wi' the moon's old glim on the grey, wet sand
An' him no more to me nor me to him
    Than the wind goin' over my hand.

Rooms

I remember rooms that have had their part
In the steady slowing down of the heart;
The room in Paris, the room at Geneva,
The little damp room with the seaweed smell,
And that ceaseless maddening sound of the tide –
    Rooms where for good or for ill, things died:
But there is the room where we two lie dead
Though every morning we seem to wake, and might just as well seem to sleep again
    As we shall some day in the other dustier quieter bed
    Out there – in the sun – in the rain.

> In the steady slowing down of the heart

The Peddler

Lend me a little while the key
    That locks your heavy heart, and I'll give you back –
Rarer than books and ribbons and beads bright to see
    This little Key of Dreams out of my pack.

The road, the road, beyond men's bolted doors,
    There shall I walk and you go free of me,
For yours lies North across the moors,
    And mine South. To what seas?

How if we stopped and let our solemn selves go by,
    While my gay ghost caught and kissed yours, as ghosts don't do,
And by the wayside, this forgotten you and I
    Sat, and were twenty-two?

Give me the key that locks your tired eyes,
    And I will lend you this one from my pack,
Brighter than coloured beads and painted books that make men wise:
    Take it. No, give it back!

Robert **Frost**

(1874–1963)

In 1912 Robert Frost, aged 38, sailed to England with his wife and four children, without a book to his credit, and with a list of frustrations and disappointments behind him. In 1915 he sailed back, an established poet. But his early lack of success coloured his sense of himself and his achievement. He was left beset with doubts.

He was born in San Francisco. His father was from New England, but a New Englander who named his son after the Confederate general Robert E. Lee (Robert Lee Frost). He lived in California until he was 11. His father died of tuberculosis and Robert, his Scottish-born mother and his sister moved to Salem, New Hampshire. Salem was a place where belonging was hard unless you were born there. It was necessary to construct an identity, and this construction might take the form of rejections and exclusions, and *refiguring* childhood.

Until he got to New England he had read almost nothing. At the age of 12 he began to acquire a taste for verse and when he graduated from High School in 1892 he was class poet. He made a few attempts at the academic world – Dartmouth, which he dropped out of to take a job in a mill; Harvard, which he left to try shoe-making, editing a local paper, and farming – before he decided to throw himself into poetry under his own supervision.

The quality of Frost's sound *in his voice, in his delivery* is astonishing. To have heard him read, or to hear recordings, is to experience an immediate adjustment of ear to his distinctive pace and cadence. He seems to speak directly, and this is due to the studied casualness of his art. There is a sense of language overheard, rural voices unencumbered by sophistication.

An English publisher took on his first book, *A Boy's Will*, in 1913. It is very English-seeming, full of archaisms, conventional poetic forms and themes. Edward Thomas recognized a wholesomeness, and 'a calm eagerness of emotion' which raised the plainness to harmonies. This is the language men might use in speaking to men, without eccentricity.

Frost was promoted into American favourite poet, a kind of 'common man' with enormous public charm, though his private life was less ordered and charmed than his admirers thought. His popular lectures helped those who didn't like verse to get a hold on it. But the world of poetry into which he drew people was not quite as they imagined it would be. Easy at one level, once inside, it was full of sinister shadows. There are voices talking, the poet transcribing, faithful to what he hears and at the same time faithful to his art. To remain faithful to the voices, he has to give them space and range; to keep faith with his art he must select, perfect, find rather than impose order. Aware of these divergent wills, the poet in the end affirms nothing apart from the fact that nothing can be affirmed. 'The figure a poem makes. It begins in delight and ends in wisdom.' When Frost says delight, he means the delight of sound, and of recognizable context, not the delight of affirmation or jollity. When he says wisdom, he means not moral lesson but human insight. Wisdom understands what is, it does not judge, it does not generalize. 'Like a piece of ice on a hot stove the poem must ride on its own melting' – a wonderful image for the making of the poem and for the reading of it.

The Runaway

Once when the snow of the year was beginning to fall,
We stopped by a mountain pasture to say, "Whose colt?"
A little Morgan had one forefoot on the wall,
The other curled at his breast. He dipped his head
And snorted at us. And then he had to bolt.
We heard the miniature thunder where he fled,
And we saw him, or thought we saw him, dim and gray,
Like a shadow against the curtain of falling flakes.
"I think the little fellow's afraid of the snow.
He isn't winter-broken. It isn't play
With the little fellow at all. He's running away.
I doubt if even his mother could tell him, 'Sakes,
It's only weather'. He'd think she didn't know!
Where is his mother? He can't be out alone."
And now he comes again with a clatter of stone,
And mounts the wall again with whited eyes
And all his tail that isn't hair up straight.
He shudders his coat as if to throw off flies.
"Whoever it is that leaves him out so late,
When other creatures have gone to stall and bin,
Ought to be told to come and take him in."

> Like a shadow against the curtain of falling flakes.

Mending Wall

Something there is that doesn't love a wall,
That sends the frozen-ground-swell under it,
And spills the upper boulders in the sun;
And makes gaps even two can pass abreast.
The work of hunters is another thing:
I have come after them and made repair
Where they have left not one stone on a stone,
But they would have the rabbit out of hiding,
To please the yelping dogs. The gaps I mean,
No one has seen them made or heard them made,
But at spring mending-time we find them there,
I let my neighbor know beyond the hill;
And on a day we meet to walk the line
And set the wall between us once again.
We keep the wall between us as we go.
To each the boulders that have fallen to each.

And some are loaves and some so nearly balls
We have to use a spell to make them balance:
'Stay where you are until our backs are turned!'
We wear our fingers rough with handling them.
Oh, just another kind of outdoor game,
One on a side. It comes to little more:
There where it is we do not need the wall:
He is all pine and I am apple orchard.
My apple trees will never get across
And eat the cones under his pines, I tell him.
He only says, 'Good fences make good neighbors.'
Spring is the mischief in me, and I wonder
If I could put a notion in his head:
'*Why* do they make good neighbors? Isn't it
Where there are cows? But here there are no cows.
Before I built a wall I'd ask to know
What I was walling in or walling out,
And to whom I was like to give offense.
Something there is that doesn't love a wall,
That wants it down.' I could say 'Elves' to him,
But it's not elves exactly, and I'd rather
He said it for himself. I see him there,
Bringing a stone grasped firmly by the top
In each hand, like an old-stone savage armed.
He moves in darkness as it seems to me,
Not of woods only and the shade of trees.
He will not go behind his father's saying,
And he likes having thought of it so well
He says again, 'Good fences make good neighbors.'

Something there is that doesn't
love a wall

Stopping by Woods on a Snowy Evening

Whose woods these are I think I know.
His house is in the village, though;
He will not see me stopping here
To watch his woods fill up with snow.

My little horse must think it queer
To stop without a farmhouse near
Between the woods and frozen lake
The darkest evening of the year.

He gives his harness bells a shake
To ask if there is some mistake.
The only other sound's the sweep
Of easy wind and downy flake.

The woods are lovely, dark and deep,
But I have promises to keep,
And miles to go before I sleep,
And miles to go before I sleep.

Mowing

There was never a sound beside the wood but one,
And that was my long scythe whispering to the ground.
What was it it whispered? I knew not well myself;
Perhaps it was something about the heat of the sun,
Something, perhaps, about the lack of sound—
And that was why it whispered and did not speak.
It was no dream of the gift of idle hours,
Or easy gold at the hand of fay or elf:
Anything more than the truth would have seemed too weak
To the earnest love that laid the swale in rows,
Not without feeble-pointed spikes of flowers
(Pale orchises), and scared a bright green snake.
The fact is the sweetest dream that labor knows.
My long scythe whispered and left the hay to make.

The Road Not Taken

Two roads diverged in a yellow wood,
And sorry I could not travel both
And be one traveler, long I stood
And looked down one as far as I could
To where it bent in the undergrowth;

Then took the other, as just as fair,
And having perhaps the better claim,
Because it was grassy and wanted wear;
Though as for that the passing there
Had worn them really about the same,

And both that morning equally lay
In leaves no step had trodden black.
Oh, I kept the first for another day!
Yet knowing how way leads on to way,
I doubted if I should ever come back.

I shall be telling this with a sigh
Somewhere ages and ages hence:
Two roads diverged in a wood, and I—
I took the one less traveled by,
And that has made all the difference.

'Out, Out –'

The buzz-saw snarled and rattled in the yard
And made dust and dropped stove-length sticks of wood,
Sweet-scented stuff when the breeze drew across it.
And from there those that lifted eyes could count
Five mountain ranges one behind the other
Under the sunset far into Vermont.
And the saw snarled and rattled, snarled and rattled,
As it ran light, or had to bear a load.
And nothing happened: day was all but done.
Call it a day, I wish they might have said
To please the boy by giving him the half hour
That a boy counts so much when saved from work.
His sister stood beside them in her apron
To tell them 'Supper'. At the word, the saw,
As if to prove saws knew what supper meant,
Leaped out at the boy's hand, or seemed to leap—
He must have given the hand. However it was,
Neither refused the meeting. But the hand!
The boy's first outcry was a rueful laugh.
As he swung toward them holding up the hand
Half in appeal, but half as if to keep
The life from spilling. Then the boy saw all—
Since he was old enough to know, big boy
Doing a man's work, though a child at heart—
He saw all spoiled. 'Don't let him cut my hand off—
The doctor, when he comes. Don't let him, sister!'
So. But the hand was gone already.
The doctor put him in the dark of ether.
He lay and puffed his lips out with his breath.
And then — the watcher at his pulse took fright.
No one believed. They listened at his heart.
Little — less — nothing! — and that ended it.
No more to build on there. And they, since they
Were not the one dead, turned to their affairs.

No more
to build on
there.

Edward
Thomas
(1878–1917)

Old Man

Rain

Lights Out

After Edward Thomas was killed in Flanders, Robert Frost wrote to Helen, the poet's widow, 'Who was ever so completely himself right up to the verge of destruction, so sure of his thought, so sure of his word?' In the present tense, he added: 'I want to see him to tell him something. I want to tell him, what I think he liked to hear from me, that he was a poet...'

Philip Edward Thomas was born in Lambeth, London, eldest of six sons. His parents' families came from Wales and he loved it, but he made the south of England, especially Wiltshire, Kent and Hampshire, his landscapes. He attended St Paul's School, Hammersmith, and went to Jesus College, Oxford. In 1897, at 19, *The Woodland Life*, his first prose book, was published. Already he and Helen were living together. They were married in 1899. They had three children.

Thomas's life, though desperately busy, was not full of incident. Three events seem crucial in retrospect. First was his meeting with Helen Noble in 1894, which led to virtual marriage when he was still an undergraduate. She provided an emotional and practical mainstay, but also – earlier than either of them intended – a family. He decided to become a writer and followed his vocation for 22 years, eking out a freelance living, reviewing, anthologizing and writing over 30 prose books on subjects ranging from the countryside to tourist guides, from literary criticism to stories, biographies, autobiographies and an autobiographical novel. Between 1910 and 1912, driven by financial necessity, he wrote no fewer than 12 of his prose books. He suffered a mental breakdown in 1911 and contemplated suicide.

Then came his meeting with Frost. In 1914 he reviewed *North of Boston* three times, saying in the first review, 'This is one of the most revolutionary books of modern times, but one of the quietest and least aggressive. It speaks, and it is poetry.' From Frost's poetry and friendship he developed the confidence to compose poems. In August 1914 he wrote to his intimate friend Eleanor Farjeon, 'I may as well write poetry. Did anyone ever begin at thirty-six in the shade?' Reading poetry had been his passion; now he set about writing the fewer than 150 poems that made his name.

War was the third event. In 1915 he enlisted in the Artists' Rifles, was made a map-reading instructor and promoted the next year to Second Lieutenant. Army service freed him from financial worry and the labour of freelancing.

When Thomas began writing prose, his style was poised and poetical, and his use of language removed from the natural voice. As more demands were made on his time, he wrote more fluently. In a letter to Eleanor Farjeon he said he was 'trying to get rid of the last rags of rhetoric and formality which left my prose so often with a dead rhythm'. Natural rhythm, which he strove for, is an extension of a natural vocabulary. Thomas wrote lines of variable length, many of them neither metrically nor syllabically regular but purely stressed in rhythm. The pressure of content, experience or occasion, determined line lengths, pauses, rhythm and extent. Even his sonnets are irregular. He is most subtle in his line endings. A poem's rhythm and syntax may seem to indicate a direction of development which, at the beginning of a new line, unexpectedly alters: syntax and line ending are counterpointed. We do not linger over a literary effect but are surprised deeper into the experience.

Old Man

Old Man, or Lads-Love, — in the name there's nothing
To one that knows not Lads-Love, or Old Man,
The hoar-green feathery herb, almost a tree,
Growing with rosemary and lavender.
Even to one that knows it well, the names
Half decorate, half perplex, the thing it is:
At least, what that is clings not to the names
In spite of time. And yet I like the names.

The herb itself I like not, but for certain
I love it, as someday the child will love it
Who plucks a feather from the door-side bush
Whenever she goes in or out of the house.
Often she waits there, snipping the tips and shrivelling
The shreds at last on to the path, perhaps
Thinking, perhaps of nothing, till she sniffs
Her fingers and runs off. The bush is still
But half as tall as she, though it is as old;
So well she clips it. Not a word she says;
And I can only wonder how much hereafter
She will remember, with that bitter scent,
Of garden rows, and ancient damson trees
Topping a hedge, a bent path to a door,
A low thick bush beside the door, and me
Forbidding her to pick.
                        As for myself,
Where first I met the bitter scent is lost.
I, too, often shrivel the grey shreds,
Sniff them and think and sniff again and try
Once more to think what it is I am remembering,
Always in vain. I cannot like the scent,
Yet I would rather give up others more sweet,
With no meaning, than this bitter one.

I have mislaid the key. I sniff the spray
And think of nothing; I see and I hear nothing;
Yet seem, too, to be listening, lying in wait
For what I should, yet never can, remember:
No garden appears, no path, no hoar-green bush
Of Lad's-love, or Old Man, no child beside,
Neither father nor mother, nor any playmate;
Only an avenue, dark, nameless, without end.

Rain

Rain, midnight rain, nothing but the wild rain
On this bleak hut, and solitude, and me
Remembering again that I shall die
And neither hear the rain nor give it thanks
For washing me cleaner than I have been
Since I was born into this solitude.
Blessed are the dead that the rain rains upon:
But here I pray that none whom once I loved
Is dying to-night or lying still awake
Solitary, listening to the rain,
Either in pain or thus in sympathy
Helpless among the living and the dead,
Like a cold water among broken reeds,
Myriads of broken reeds all still and stiff,
Like me who have no love which this wild rain
Has not dissolved except the love of death,
If love it be for what is perfect and
Cannot, the tempest tells me, disappoint.

> Blessed are
> the dead that
> the rain rains
> upon

Lights Out

I have come to the borders of sleep,
The unfathomable deep
Forest where all must lose
Their way, however straight,
Or winding, soon or late;
They cannot choose.

Many a road and track
That, since the dawn's first crack,
Up to the forest brink,
Deceived the travellers,
Suddenly now blurs,
And in they sink.

Here love ends,
Despair, ambition ends;
All pleasure and all trouble,
Although most sweet or bitter,
Here ends in sleep that is sweeter
Than tasks most noble.

There is not any book
Or face of dearest look
That I would not turn from now
To go into the unknown
I must enter, and leave, alone,
I know not how.

The tall forest towers;
Its cloudy foliage lowers
Ahead, shelf above shelf;
Its silence I hear and obey
That I may lose my way
And myself.

Wallace **Stevens**

(1879–1955)

The Idea of Order at Key West

The Emperor of Ice-Cream

Thirteen Ways of Looking at a Blackbird

The Snow Man

Final Soliloquy of the Interior Paramour

No war shook the foundations of Wallace Stevens's imaginative world, though two World Wars happened some way off, shaking the Europe from which he ordered beautiful books, prints and pictures, but never visited. He had correspondents – it would be too much to call them friends – and when they sent him a new book to read he might reply: 'Reading one's friends books is a good deal like kissing their wives, I suppose. The less said about it, the better.' The friends' wives that he actually kissed, chastely, were generally business associates. In 1916 he joined the Hartford Accident and Indemnity Company, Hartford, Connecticut, of which he became Vice-President in 1934 and with which he remained until his death.

Stevens was born in Reading, Pennyslvania, of Dutch extraction on his mother's side. His father was a lawyer. He studied at Harvard from 1897 to 1900, and then at New York Law School, and was admitted to the bar in 1904. He started practising law, and married in 1909.

He began writing poetry reticently in his teens. It was not until he was 35 that – first as Peter Parasol, then in his own name – he published poems in magazines. His first collection, *Harmonium*, appeared when he was 44 (1923). His second, *Ideas of Order*, followed 12 years later. After that there was a flow of books, culminating in *Collected Poems* in 1954, and a book of essays, *The Necessary Angel: Essays on Reality and Imagination*, published three years before. Significant work appeared after his death in *Opus Posthumous*.

Stevens loves the long poem and repeating metrical patterns precisely, while altering the language they contain. The diction causes us to linger over his words, we are not allowed to rush ahead. It is possible to read Stevens for years with intense pleasure and never to care what the poems mean because the sense of sense is so strong and the movement of feeling so assured. If we do question his meanings and try to tie the poems in to them, we may displace the poetry itself. The subtlety of his thought is less compelling than the magic of his effects on the ear and the eye, his ability to rouse the 'intellectual emotions'.

He knew other writers – William Carlos Williams, e.e. cummings, Marianne Moore. They knew him and his work. He was part of the group, but always off on the fringe, a luminous absence. That's where he wanted to be. He never invited a literary friend to his house. Donald Davie regarded Stevens as a reactionary, a neo-Romantic: 'a Keatsian allegiance is the clue' to him. The critic Hugh Kenner regards his as 'an Edward Lear poetic, pushed toward all limits', a master of the seeming sense which, closely examined, is nonsense. These judgements tell a part truth but sell short one of the most pleasurable poets of the twentieth century. He owed as large a debt to Walt Whitman as Ezra Pound did, and, like Pound, Eliot and Yeats, he was influenced by French, Italian and German poetry. Stevens deliberately chose pre-modern forms for his poems knowing that modern verse was challenging these forms. This choice placed him, paradoxically, at the heart of the modern. He wanted his poetry to hold not an historical, political, theological or contingent world but a world unassistedly 'real', made in and out of language.

The Idea of Order at Key West

She sang beyond the genius of the sea.
The water never formed to mind or voice,
Like a body wholly body, fluttering
Its empty sleeves; and yet its mimic motion
Made constant cry, caused constantly a cry,
That was not ours although we understood,
Inhuman, of the veritable ocean.

The sea was not a mask. No more was she.
The song and water were not medleyed sound
Even if what she sang was what she heard,
Since what she sang was uttered word by word.
It may be that in all her phrases stirred
The grinding water and the gasping wind;
But it was she and not the sea we heard.

For she was the maker of the song she sang.
The ever-hooded, tragic-gestured sea
Was merely a place by which she walked to sing.
Whose spirit is this? we said, because we knew
It was the spirit that we sought and knew
That we should ask this often as she sang.

If it was only the dark voice of the sea
That rose, or even colored by many waves;
If it was only the outer voice of sky
And cloud, of the sunken coral water-walled,
However clear, it would have been deep air,
The heaving speech of air, a summer sound
Repeated in a summer without end
And sound alone. But it was more than that,
More even than her voice, and ours, among
The meaningless plungings of water and the wind,
Theatrical distances, bronze shadows heaped
On high horizons, mountainous atmospheres
Of sky and sea.
                    It was her voice that made
The sky acutest at its vanishing.
She measured to the hour its solitude.

She was the single artificer of the world
In which she sang. And when she sang, the sea,
Whatever self it had, became the self
That was her song, for she was the maker. Then we,
As we beheld her striding there alone,
Knew that there never was a world for her
Except the one she sang and, singing, made.

Ramon Fernandez, tell me, if you know,
Why, when the singing ended and we turned
Toward the town, tell why the glassy lights,
The lights in the fishing boats at anchor there,
As the night descended, tilting in the air,
Mastered the night and portioned out the sea,
Fixing emblazoned zones and fiery poles,
Arranging, deepening, enchanting night.

Oh! Blessed rage for order, pale Ramon,
The maker's rage to order words of the sea,
Words of the fragrant portals, dimly-starred,
And of ourselves and our origins,
In ghostlier demarcations, keener sounds.

The Emperor of Ice-Cream

Call the roller of big cigars,
The muscular one, and bid him whip
In kitchen cups concupiscent curds.
Let the wenches dawdle in such dress
As they are used to wear, and let the boys
Bring flowers in last month's newspapers.
Let be be finale of seem.
The only emperor is the emperor of ice-cream.

Take from the dresser of deal,
Lacking the three glass knobs, that sheet
On which she embroidered fantails once
And spread it so as to cover her face.
If her horny feet protrude, they come
To show how cold she is, and dumb.
Let the lamp affix its beam.
The only emperor is the emperor of ice-cream.

Thirteen Ways of Looking at a Blackbird

I   Among twenty snowy mountains,
    The only moving thing
    Was the eye of the black bird.

II   I was of three minds,
     Like a tree
     In which there are three blackbirds.

III   The blackbird whirled in the autumn winds.
      It was a small part of the pantomime.

IV   A man and a woman
     Are one.
     A man and a woman and a blackbird
     Are one.

V   I do not know which to prefer,
    The beauty of inflections
    Or the beauty of innuendoes,
    The blackbird whistling
    Or just after.

VI   Icicles filled the long window
     With barbaric glass.
     The shadow of the blackbird
     Crossed it, to and fro.
     The mood
     Traced in the shadow
     An indecipherable cause.

VII   O thin men of Haddam,
      Why do you imagine golden birds?
      Do you not see how the blackbird
      Walks around the feet
      Of the women about you?

VIII   I know noble accents
       And lucid, inescapable rhythms;
       But I know, too,
       That the blackbird is involved
       In what I know.

IX   When the blackbird flew out of sight,
     It marked the edge
     Of one of many circles.

X   At the sight of blackbirds
    Flying in a green light,
    Even the bawds of euphony
    Would cry out sharply.

XI   He rode over Connecticut
     In a glass coach.
     Once, a fear pierced him,
     In that he mistook
     The shadow of his equipage
     For blackbirds.

XII   The river is moving.
      The blackbird must be flying.

XIII   It was evening all afternoon.
       It was snowing
       And it was going to snow.
       The blackbird sat
       In the cedar-limbs.

It was snowing
And it was
going to snow.

The Snow Man

One must have a mind of winter
To regard the frost and the boughs
Of the pine-trees crusted with snow;

And have been cold a long time
To behold the junipers shagged with ice,
The spruces rough in the distant glitter

Of the January sun; and not to think
Of any misery in the sound of the wind,
In the sound of a few leaves,

Which is the sound of the land
Full of the same wind
That is blowing in the same bare place

For the listener, who listens in the snow,
And, nothing himself, beholds
Nothing that is not there and the nothing that is.

> Nothing that is
> not there and the
> nothing that is.

Final Soliloquy of the Interior Paramour

Light the first light of evening, as in a room
In which we rest and, for small reason, think
The world imagined is the ultimate good.

This is, therefore, the intensest rendezvous.
It is in that thought that we collect ourselves,
Out of all the indifferences, into one thing:

Within a single thing, a single shawl
Wrapped tightly round us, since we are poor, a warmth,
A light, a power, the miraculous influence.

Here, now, we forget each other and ourselves.
We feel the obscurity of an order, a whole,
A knowledge, that which arranged the rendezvous,

Within its vital boundary, in the mind.
We say God and the imagination are one...
How high that highest candle lights the dark.

Out of this same light, out of the central mind,
We make a dwelling in the evening air,
In which being there together is enough.

William Carlos
Williams
(1883–1963)

The Red Wheelbarrow

This is just to say

Landscape with the Fall of Icarus

The Hunters in the Snow

The Great Figure

William Carlos Williams combined vocations. He was a medical doctor and a poet. When he qualified as a doctor at the University of Pennyslvania in 1906, he was already writing poetry, having started suddenly, around the age of 18. In his *Autobiography* he calls his first poem 'a bolt from the blue'; it 'broke a spell of disillusion and suicidal despondence'. Its four lines filled him with 'soul-satisfying joy' stronger than the self-criticism that followed.

A black, black cloud
flew over the sun
driven by fierce flying
rain.

In this effort his characteristics are already present: short lines, free verse (which he never called 'free', inventing the 'variable foot' to define his practice), the clear image. About 20 years later, reviewing his *Kora in Hell* (1921), Marianne Moore said: 'Compression, color, speed, accuracy and that restraint of instinctive craftsmanship which precludes anything dowdy or labored – it is essentially these qualities that we have in his work.'

He was born in Rutherford, New Jersey (his father was a travelling perfume salesman and he was raised by his mother and grandmother), and he returned to Rutherford after his studies at Leipzig and his travels in Europe, marrying his long-standing (and later long-suffering) fiancée Florence Herman, the Flossie of the poems, in 1912. He was already a close friend of H.D. (Hilda Doolittle) and of Ezra Pound, with whom he stayed in London. Pound introduced him to Yeats. He divided his life B.C. (before Pound) and A.D. after their friendship began. A decade later he revisited Europe, meeting Pound – and James Joyce.

Pound included him in his anthology *Des Imagistes* and Williams remained closer to the original imagist practice of using precise images than most of the poets in Pound's book, including Pound himself. He was not content with the small imagist poem, time after time attempting extended works. He developed an aversion to T.S. Eliot, that 'renegade American' who threw in his lot with the old culture. *The Waste Land* was a 'catastrophe' not only because of its stylistic choices but because it was so darned negative. Frost he found a hick a stage American not the real thing.

He wrote in the evenings or in his surgery between appointments, punching away at his typewriter. He tended to compose straight onto the typewriter, rather than type up poems drafted by hand. At weekends he sometimes went to New York to meet artists and writers.

He cast a spell on his contemporaries and successors. Robert Lowell revered him. Allen Ginsberg regarded himself as a disciple (Williams wrote an introduction to Ginsberg's first book). Charles Olson believed himself to have received from the master the divine fire. Adrienne Rich found his example enabling in her difficult, decisive transition.

'A poem,' he wrote, 'is a small (or large) machine made of words as [the poet] finds them inter-related about him and composes them – without distortion which would mar their exact significance – into an intense expression of his preoccupations and ardors that they may constitute a revelation in the speech that he uses.'

The Red Wheelbarrow

so much depends
upon

a red wheel
barrow

glazed with rain
water

beside the white
chickens.

glazed with rain
water

This is just to say

I have eaten
the plums
that were in
the icebox

and which
you were probably
saving
for breakfast

Forgive me
they were delicious
so sweet
and so cold

so sweet
and so cold

Landscape with the Fall of Icarus

According to Brueghel
when Icarus fell
it was spring

a farmer was ploughing
his field
the whole pageantry

of the year was
awake tingling
near

the edge of the sea
concerned
with itself

sweating in the sun
that melted
the wings' wax

unsignificantly
off the coast
there was

a splash quite unnoticed
this was
Icarus drowning

The Hunters in the Snow

The over-all picture is winter
icy mountains
in the background the return

from the hunt it is toward evening
from the left
sturdy hunters lead in

their pack the inn-sign
hanging from a
broken hinge is a stag a crucifix

between his antlers the cold
inn yard is
deserted but for a huge bonfire

that flares wind-driven tended by
women who cluster
about it to the right beyond

the hill is a pattern of skaters
Brueghel the painter
concerned with it all has chosen

a winter-struck bush for his
foreground to
complete the picture .   .

the hill is a
pattern of skaters

The Great Figure

Among the rain
and lights
I saw the figure 5
in gold
on a red
firetruck
moving
tense
unheeded
to gong clangs
siren howls
and wheels rumbling
through the dark city.

D.H.
Lawrence
(1885–1930)

David Herbert Lawrence is better known as a novelist than as a poet, yet his poems have had an impact on the life of poetry in English. Their originality anticipates much that was to follow in the aftermath of the Second World War.

The poet was born in Eastwood, Nottingham, the fourth child in his family. His father was a coal-miner, his mother a former schoolteacher. The tension between his parents is evoked in certain early lines: 'Outside the house an ash-tree hung its terrible whips.' Inside, voices rose and fell. Lawrence as a young man felt close to his mother, who died in 1910 and for whom he wrote elegies in prose and verse. In time he came to understand his father's harder perspectives. His imagination is full of contrasts: between his father's class values and his mother's middle-class hankering; between the rural and industrial landscapes that coexisted around him; between sexual and moral obligations which often seemed, in those early years, at odds. A further complication was that in childhood he was diagnosed with the lung infection which was to kill him.

From local council school he gained a scholarship to attend Nottingham High School. At the age of 16 he began work as a clerk in a surgical appliances firm at 13 shillings a week. He left to follow in his mother's footsteps by becoming a pupil teacher. At 18 he went to University College, Nottingham. Until 1912 he taught school exasperatedly, all the while working on his first novel and writing poems which began to appear in that year. With his novel *The White Peacock* he wiped the chalk dust from his fingers and went abroad for the first time, a writer.

Self-discovery involved Lawrence in running away in 1914 with Frieda von Richthofen, the German wife of a Nottingham professor. This romance has become legendary, though legend sometimes omits the fact that Frieda lost contact with her children and that she and her lover had a volatile and reposeless love. Together they travelled, sustaining one another in flight from critical and moral opprobrium at home, and in flight from death.

After the First World War, Lawrence and Frieda, tired of an England which was hostile to his artistic mission, travelled widely. He wrote travel books, essays, introductions, novels and poems. He painted. Wherever he travelled – to Italy, Australia, New Zealand, the South Seas, California, Mexico and New Mexico – he strove to be present in the place, not registering it as a visitor with a camera but apprehending it on the pulse through landscape, art and literature. He spent his last four years travelling through Europe trying to retard the development of the illness he refused to acknowledge was tuberculosis. He died in a sanatorium in the south of France.

His social and intellectual background set him apart from the writers of the day. Without academic and financial advantages, emerging from a turbulent home, he is earnest, unironic, direct – always *in* his writing – and he makes no bones about it. Not for him the fictionalized voice. He does not pose, posture or put on a mask. Perhaps his largest artistic risk was to take his writing in such deadly earnest, and to ask us to do so too. In *Nettles* (1929) and much of the later work there is unripeness, immaturity of sentiment and thought, and the occasional marring petulance of the vestigial brat. The very last poems and the best of the animal and flower poems have a serene assurance free of such blemishes.

Snake

A snake came to my water-trough
On a hot, hot day, and I in pyjamas for the heat,
To drink there.

In the deep, strange-scented shade of the great dark carob-tree
I came down the steps with my pitcher
And must wait, must stand and wait, for there he was at the trough before me.

He reached down from a fissure in the earth-wall in the gloom
And trailed his yellow-brown slackness soft-bellied down, over the edge of
        the stone trough
And rested his throat upon the stone bottom,
And where the water had dripped from the tap, in a small clearness,
He sipped with his straight mouth,
Softly drank through his straight gums, into his slack long body,
Silently.

Someone was before me at my water-trough,
And I, like a second comer, waiting.

He lifted his head from his drinking, as cattle do,
And looked at me vaguely, as drinking cattle do,
And flickered his two-forked tongue from his lips, and mused a moment,
And stooped and drank a little more,
Being earth-brown, earth-golden from the burning bowels of the earth
On the day of Sicilian July, with Etna smoking.

The voice of my education said to me
He must be killed,
For in Sicily the black, black snakes are innocent, the gold are venomous.

And voices in me said, If you were a man
You would take a stick and break him now, and finish him off.

But must I confess how I liked him,
How glad I was he had come like a guest in quiet, to drink at my water-trough
And depart peaceful, pacified, and thankless,
Into the burning bowels of this earth?

Was it cowardice, that I dared not kill him?
Was it perversity, that I longed to talk to him?
Was it humility, to feel so honoured?
I felt so honoured.

And yet those voices:
If you were not afraid, you would kill him!

And truly I was afraid, I was most afraid,
But even so, honoured still more
That he should seek my hospitality
From out the dark door of the secret earth.

He drank enough
And lifted his head, dreamily, as one who has drunken,
And flickered his tongue like a forked night on the air, so black;
Seeming to lick his lips,
And looked around like a god, unseeing, into the air,
And slowly turned his head,
And slowly, very slowly, as if thrice adream,
Proceeded to draw his slow length curving round
And climb again the broken bank of my wall-face.
And as he put his head into that dreadful hole,
And as he slowly drew up, snake-easing his shoulders, and entered farther,
A sort of horror, a sort of protest against his withdrawing into that horrid black hole,
Deliberately going into the blackness, and slowly drawing himself after,
Overcame me now his back was turned.

I looked round, I put down my pitcher,
I picked up a clumsy log
And threw it at the water-trough with a clatter.

I think it did not hit him,
But suddenly that part of him that was left behind convulsed in undignified haste,
Writhed like lightning, and was gone
Into the black hole, the earth-lipped fissure in the wall-front,
At which, in the intense still noon, I stared with fascination.

And immediately I regretted it.
I thought how paltry, how vulgar, what a mean act!
I despised myself and the voices of my accursèd human education.
And I thought of the albatross
And I wished he would come back, my snake.

For he seemed to me again like a king,
Like a king in exile, uncrowned in the underworld,
Now due to be crowned again.

And so, I missed my chance with one of the lords
Of life.
And I have something to expiate;
A pettiness.

Ezra
Pound (1885–1972)

Born in Hailey, Idaho, Ezra Pound grew up in Wyncott, Pennsylvania and became a student of Romance Languages at the University of Pennsylvania. His contemporaries included William Carlos Williams and H.D. (Hilda Doolittle) whom he courted, but her father thought him a poor match. After graduation in 1906 he taught briefly, but was dismissed as too bohemian for Wabash College. He travelled to Venice, publishing his first book, *A Lume Spento*, at his own expense. He loved the lush excesses of Algernon Charles Swinburne's poetry, the posed emotionalism of Dante Gabriel Rossetti's, and Robert Browning's invented voices. Walt Whitman was in his blood. He was translating the poetry of the troubadours, Provençal and Anglo-Saxon verse. Everything he read was 'laid down' for eventual decanting into his most ambitious work, the *Cantos*.

He busied himself about other writers' careers, too, including Yeats's, H.D.'s, Williams's and Eliot's. He invented the Imagists and then the Vorticists, polemical 'movements' to underline the nature of Modernist experiment and to assemble groups of newfangled writers, different in culture and background from those who ran the establishment, to challenge the conventional order of things.

More important than movements was his engagement with other languages. Already in *Lustra* (1913) there were oriental touches, and by the time *Cathay* was published (1915) the lessons of Chinese poetry and drama were deeply embedded. His translations or imitations of Chinese verse are included, his most compelling versions of any poetry apart from the long, unexcerptable *Homage to Sextus Propertius* (1917). Pound 'internalized' the 'music'. 'To break the pentameter, that was the first heave', he said elsewhere.

In *Hugh Selwyn Mauberley*, published in 1920, in variable rhymed quatrains, he discarded the last remnants of the 1890s. Eliot read the poem as 'a document of an epoch', and it deserves to be placed beside his *The Waste Land*, with which it shares themes and techniques. The quatrains break down in the fourth and fifth sections included here, and in free verse Pound writes one of the great war poems, prefiguring the clarity and anger of the *Cantos*. The theme of usury first appears in *Mauberley*. It becomes an eloquent ('With usura hath no man a house of good stone', Canto XLV) and then a poisoned strand in the *Cantos*, the strand upon which hangs his notorious anti-Semitism.

In 1914 Pound had married Dorothy Shakespear. In 1920 they moved to Paris and in 1924 to Italy, where they settled in Rapallo. There he stayed for much of the rest of his life, apart from his incarceration first at Pisa and then in a mental hospital after the Second World War. Before he left England he had already begun the *Cantos*, a work which became all consuming. In 1925 he revised and published *XVI Cantos*, to which at intervals further batches were added, the last as *Drafts and Fragments* (1968), four years before the poet, who had fallen silent, died.

As Donald Davie says, for those who value the *Cantos* the poetry must 'survive a self-evidently and perilously wrong understanding of history, and hence of politics'. It must also survive the huge wealth of reference, of disparate-seeming traditions, which inform it: Chinese ideograms, quotes from Thomas Jefferson, Provençal, Italian, Greek, and a host of other cultural 'zones'. Pound more clearly than any of his contemporaries illustrates the complete change in attitudes to 'tradition' that occurs when form and language are used in entirely new ways. After Pound we read poetry differently. If, that is, we 'read' Pound at all.

Speech for Psyche in the Golden Book of Apuleius

All night, and as the wind lieth among
The cypress trees, he lay,
Nor held me save as air that brusheth by one
Close, and as the petals of flowers falling
Waver and seem not drawn to earth, so he
Seemed over me to hover light as leaves
And closer me than air,
And music flowing through me seemed to open
Mine eyes upon new colours.
O winds, what wind can match the weight of him!

> Close, and as the petals of
> flowers falling

From Hugh Selwyn Mauberley

IV
These fought in any case,
and some believing,
                    pro domo, in any case …

Some quick to arm,
some for adventure,
some from fear of weakness,
some from fear of censure,
some for love of slaughter, in imagination,
learning later …
some in fear, learning love of slaughter;

Died some pro patria,
                    non 'dulce' non 'et decor' …
walked eye-deep in hell
believing in old men's lies, then unbelieving
came home, home to a lie,
home to many deceits,
home to old lies and new infamy;
usury age-old and age-thick
and liars in public places.

Daring as never before, wastage as never before.
Young blood and high blood,
Fair cheeks, and fine bodies;

fortitude as never before

frankness as never before,
disillusions as never told in the old
          days,
hysterias, trench confessions,
laughter out of dead bellies.

V
There died a myriad,
And of the best, among them,
For an old bitch gone in the teeth,
For a botched civilization,

Charm, smiling at the good mouth,
Quick eyes gone under earth's lid,

For two gross of broken statues,
For a few thousand battered books.

The River Merchant's Wife: A Letter
By Rihaku (Li T'ai Po)

While my hair was still cut straight across my forehead
I played about the front gate, pulling flowers.
You came by on bamboo stilts, playing horse,
You walked about my seat, playing with blue plums.
And we went on living in the village of Chōkan:
Two small people, without dislike or suspicion.

At fourteen I married My Lord you.
I never laughed, being bashful.
Lowering my head, I looked at the wall.
Called to, a thousand times, I never looked back.

At fifteen I stopped scowling,
I desired my dust to be mingled with yours
Forever and forever and forever.
Why should I climb the look out?

At sixteen you departed,
You went into far Ku-tō-en, by the river of swirling eddies,
And you have been gone five months.
The monkeys make sorrowful noise overhead.

You dragged your feet when you went out.
By the gate now, the moss is grown, the different mosses,
Too deep to clear them away!
The leaves fall early this autumn, in wind.
The paired butterflies are already yellow with August
Over the grass in the west garden;
They hurt me. I grow older.
If you are coming down through the narrows of the river Kiang,
Please let me know beforehand,
And I will come out to meet you
                    As far as Chō-fū-Sa.

I desired my dust to be mingled with yours
Forever and forever and forever.

From Canto LXXXI

Libretto

Yet

Ere the season died a-cold

Borne upon a zephyr's shoulder

I rose through the aureate sky

Lawes and Jenkyns guard thy rest

Dolmetsch ever be thy guest,

Has he tempered the viol's wood

To enforce   both the grave   and the acute?

Has he curved us the bowl of the lute?

Lawes and Jenkyns guard thy rest

Dolmetsch ever be thy guest

Hast 'ou fashioned so airy a mood

To draw up leaf from the root?

Hast 'ou found   a cloud   so light

As seemed neither mist nor shade?

Then resolve me, tell me aright

If Waller sang or Dowland played,

Your eyen two wol sleye me sodenly

I may the beauté of hem nat susteyne

And for 180 years almost nothing.

Ed ascoltando al leggier mormorio

there came new subtlety of eyes into my tent,

whether of spirit or hypostasis,

but what the blindfold hides

or at carneval

nor any pair showed anger

Saw but the eyes and stance between the eyes,

colour, diastasis,

careless or unaware it had not the

whole tent's room

nor was place for the full Ειδως

interpass, penetrate

casting but shade beyond the other lights

sky's clear

night's sea

green of the mountain pool

shone from the unmasked eyes in half-mask's space.

What thou lovest well remains,

the rest is dross

sky's clear
night's sea
green of the
mountain pool

What thou lov'st well shall not be reft from thee
What thou lov'st well is thy true heritage
Whose world, or mine or theirs
                                        or is it of none?
First came the seen, thus the palpable
    Elysium, though it were in the halls of hell,
What thou lovest well is thy true heritage
What thou lov'st well shall not be reft from thee

The ant's a centaur in his dragon world.
Pull down thy vanity, it is not man
Made courage, or made order, or made grace,
    Pull down thy vanity, I say pull down.
Learn of the green world what can be thy place
In scaled invention or true artistry,
Pull down thy vanity,
                            Paquin pull down!
The green casque has outdone your elegance.

"Master thyself, then others shall thee beare"
    Pull down thy vanity
Thou art a beaten dog beneath the hail,
A swollen magpie in a fitful sun,
Half black half white
Nor knowst'ou wing from tail
Pull down thy vanity
        How mean thy hates
Fostered in falsity,
        Pull down thy vanity,
Rathe to destroy, niggard in charity,
Pull down thy vanity,
        I say pull down.

But to have done instead of not doing
        this is not vanity
To have, with decency, knocked
That a Blunt should open
    To have gathered from the air a live tradition
or from a fine old eye the unconquered flame
This is not vanity.
    Here error is all in the not done,
all in the diffidence that faltered,

Robinson
Jeffers (1887–1962)

Viewed in the company of the Modernists, Robinson Jeffers is an austere figure. He re-invents America as a vigorous, testing wilderness, hostile to the seductions of the metropolis and to any artistic or political stance which is not *independent*.

He was born in Pittsburgh, Pennsylvania. His father, a professor of Old Testament literature and a Presbyterian minister, set his child to learning Greek when he was five (the poet later translated Euripides' *Medea*). In 1903 the family moved to California, where he studied medicine, and then forestry, at Occidental College. In 1912, after a legacy, he became a man of independent means, married in 1913 his 'hawk-like' wife Una, and began quarrying and gathering from the beach the granite for his legendary house and tower at a rugged site at Carmel on the Monterey coast. Having built his fortress, he seldom left it. In a world of war, depressions and violent dislocations, it was his point of permanence and his recurrent subject. He called his approach 'inhumanism', anticipating mankind's extinction. Walt Whitman's lavishly populous poetry is emptied out by Jeffers, whose long lines recall Whitman's and share certain Biblical sources, but are remote from Whitman's overwhelming warm-heartedness in theme. Jeffers's long narrative poems enact man's vexed and uncomprehending relationship with nature.

He has advocates who present him as a radical eco-poet. Certainly the politics that follow from his vision underline some of the human risks of green ideology. Others see him as the poet of extreme individualism. His publishers during the Second World War saw fit to dissociate themselves from his spectacularly hostile politics in the blurb to his collected poems. Most discerning readers value him, not for his ideas, but for the compelling power of his narrative, its brisk movement and direct unapologetic expression of different aspects of human desire. It moves, not without melodrama, through recurrent themes of incest, lust and cursed heredity. 'I decided not to tell lies in verse. Not to feign any emotion that I did not feel.' His shorter poems are impassioned, too.

He has distinctive qualities and represents one of several culminations, or closings-down, of Whitman's line. He is a reactionary, anti-Modernist pole in American poetry, yet his technique has been shaped and toned by Modernism; just as much as Pound he knows the Greeks; just as much as Lawrence he knows the Bible. 'The poets lie too much,' he says. In saying this, he claims to be telling the truth. But he is as much a liar as the rest of them because of the partiality of his vision. He wrote some exceptional poems which evoke a primeval nature that he engages in body and mind, or which level a savage, prophetic, elegiac beam of language at America. He seems to relish pain, storm, suffering, not because they cleanse but because they are a value in themselves; he celebrates death and the nature that survives it. 'You and I, Cassandra,' he says with his towering virtue. The sound of the sea and the smell of his mountains are his elected elements. Like one of his hawks he had a singular nature; he also had a rare freedom in that, like some of the great poets of the nineteenth century, he was emancipated by a private income from certain common, humanizing forms of social engagement.

Shine, Perishing Republic

While this America settles in the mould of its vulgarity, heavily thickening
    to empire,
And protest, only a bubble in the molten mass, pops and sighs out, and the
    mass hardens,

I sadly smiling remember that the flower fades to make fruit, the fruit rots
    to make earth.
Out of the mother; and through the spring exultances, ripeness and
    decadence; and home to the mother.

You making haste haste on decay: not blameworthy; life is good, be it
    stubbornly long or suddenly
A mortal splendor: meteors are not needed less than mountains: shine, perishing republic.

But for my children, I would have them keep their distance from the
    thickening center; corruption
Never has been compulsory, when the cities lie at the monster's feet there
    are left the mountains.

And boys, be in nothing so moderate as in love of man, a clever servant,
    insufferable master.
There is the trap that catches noblest spirits, that caught – they say –
God, when he walked on earth.

It is time for us to kiss the earth again

Return

A little too abstract, a little too wise,
It is time for us to kiss the earth again,
It is time to let the leaves rain from the skies,
Let the rich life run to the roots again.
I will go to the lovely Sur Rivers
And dip my arms in them up to the shoulders.
I will find my accounting where the alder leaf quivers
In the ocean wind over the river boulders.
I will touch things and things and no more thoughts,
That breed like mouthless May-flies darkening the sky,
The insect clouds that blind our passionate hawks
So that they cannot strike, hardly can fly.
Things are the hawk's food and noble is the mountain, Oh noble
Pico Blanco, steep sea-wave of marble.

Fire on the Hills

The deer were bounding like blown leaves
Under the smoke in front the roaring wave of the brush-fire;
I thought of the smaller lives that were caught.
Beauty is not always lovely; the fire was beautiful, the terror
Of the deer was beautiful; and when I returned
Down the back slopes after the fire had gone by, an eagle
Was perched on the jag of a burnt pine,
Insolent and gorged, cloaked in the folded storms of his shoulders.
He had come from far off for the good hunting
With fire for his beater to drive the game; the sky was merciless
Blue, and the hills merciless black,
The sombre-feathered great bird sleepily merciless between them.
I thought, painfully, but the whole mind,
The destruction that brings an eagle from heaven is better than mercy.

The Stars Go Over the Lonely Ocean

Unhappy about some far off things
That are not my affair, wandering
Along the coast and up the lean ridges,
I saw in the evening
The stars go over the lonely ocean,
And a black-maned wild boar
Plowing with his snout on Mal Paso Mountain.

The old monster snuffled, "Here are sweet roots,
Fat grubs, slick beetles and sprouted acorns.
The best nation in Europe has fallen,
And that is Finland,
But the stars go over the lonely ocean,"
The old black-bristled boar,
Tearing the sod on Mal Paso Mountain.

"The world's in a bad way, my man,
And bound to be worse before it mends;
Better lie up in the mountain here
Four or five centuries,
While the stars go over the lonely ocean,"
Said the old father of wild pigs,
Plowing the fallow on Mal Paso Mountain.

"Keep clear of the dupes that talk
       democracy
And the dogs that talk revolution,
Drunk with talk, liars and believers.
I believe in my tusks.
Long live freedom and damn the
       ideologies,"
Said the gamey black-maned wild boar
Tusking the turf on Mal Paso Mountain.

Marianne
Moore
(1887–1972)

To a Snail

What Are Years?

The Mind is an Enchanting Thing

Wallace Stevens called her 'A Poet that Matters'. 'The tall pages of *Selected Poems* by Marianne Moore are the papers of a scrupulous spirit,' he says, 'unaffected, witty, colloquial'. But Moore is affected, often delightfully so: her art is wilful in terms of form and language, filled with surprises and clarities. The surprises are in the world and in language: she is a most self-effacing writer.

She was born in St Louis, Missouri. From her father, a Presbyterian minister, she learned to be a moralist, though her morality is neither orthodox nor dogmatic. Like him she 'believed in' family (though she never started one of her own) and individual social responsibility. From her mother she derived a sense of phrasing and her 'thought or pith'. She studied at Bryn Mawr College, and then learned to be a typist.

From 1915 onwards she published verse in magazines and was friendly with Ezra Pound and William Carlos Williams. In 1921, without her prior knowledge, friends published her first book, *Poems*. Three years later she added work and republished the volume as *Observations*. She received numerous prizes and in 1935 T. S. Eliot published her *Selected Poems*. Her *Collected Poems* first appeared in 1951. She translated *La Fontaine's Fables* inventively, if laboriously.

Moore was a lady of hats. A friend, remembering her, wrote: 'She once began a story with "I was leaving Boston wearing two hats…". I can't remember the story itself, I was too much taken up with the preamble. The hats were obviously too big to pack. I think the tricorne was the first classic hat and the big flat-brimmed one was more often worn later.' He remembers how, when he visited her in Brooklyn, 'she sent me two dollars to pay for the journey from my New York hotel'. Her conversation was 'sharp and even acerbic'; beneath the decorous exterior there was something 'richer and less restricted'. Most of her adult life she spent in New York (a flat in Greenwich Village, then in lower Manhattan) and Brooklyn (to be near her brother, a Navy chaplain).

She was learned but modest about her learning and never built a theory of literature or issued manifestos – she never shouted. Her poem 'Poetry', originally five stanzas, 30 lines, she pruned down to three famous lines:

I, too, dislike it.
> Reading it, however, with a perfect contempt for it, one discovers in
> it, after all, a place for the genuine.

'One would rather disguise than travesty emotion; give away a nice thing than sell it; dismember a garment of rich aesthetic construction than degrade it to the utilitarian offices of the boneyard.' Moore pursues what she calls 'disinterested ends', and is willing to identify without identifying with, to draw without faking the lines for effect. Her reading voice meticulously conveys the architecture of the verse, as sound and syntax.

To a Snail

If "compression is the first grace of style,"
you have it. Contractility is a virtue
as modesty is a virtue.
It is not the acquisition of any one thing
that is able to adorn,
or the incidental quality that occurs
as a concomitant of something well said,
that we value in style,
but the principle that is hid:
in the absence of feet, "a method of conclusions";
"a knowledge of principles,"
in the curious phenomenon of your occipital horn.

What Are Years?

What is our innocence,
what is our guilt? All are
    naked, none is safe. And whence
is courage: the unanswered question,
the resolute doubt, —
dumbly calling, deafly listening—that
in misfortune, even death,
        encourage others
        and in its defeat, stirs

    the soul to be strong? He
sees deep and is glad, who
        accedes to mortality
and in his imprisonment rises
upon himself as
the sea in a chasm, struggling to be
free and unable to be,
        in its surrendering
        finds its continuing.

    So he who strongly feels,
behaves. The very bird,
    grown taller as he sings, steels
his form straight up. Though he is captive,
his mighty singing
says, satisfaction is a lowly
thing, how pure a thing is joy.
        This is mortality,
        this is eternity.

in its
surrendering
finds its
continuing.

The Mind is an Enchanting Thing

is an enchanted thing
        like the glaze on a
katydid-wing
                subdivided by sun
                till the nettings are legion.
Like Gieseking playing Scarlatti;

like the apteryx-awl
        as a beak, or the
kiwi's rain-shawl
                of haired feathers, the mind
                feeling its way as though blind,
walks along with its eyes on the ground.

It has memory's ear
        that can hear without
having to hear.
                Like the gyroscope's fall,
                truly equivocal
because trued by regnant certainty,

it is a power of
        strong enchantment. It
is like the dove-
                neck animated by
                sun; it is memory's eye;
                it's conscientious inconsistency.

It tears off the veil; tears
        the temptation, the
mist the heart wears,
                from its eyes — if the heart
                has a face; it takes apart
dejection. It's fire in the dove-neck's

iridescence; in the
        inconsistencies
of Scarlatti.
                Unconfusion submits
                its confusion to proof; it's
not a Herod's oath that cannot change.

Like the
gyroscope's fall,
truly equivocal

T.S. Eliot

(1888–1965)

La Figlia Che Piange
The Love Song of J. Alfred Prufrock

T.S. Eliot insists on the poet's impersonality. The critic Hugh Kenner calls him 'the invisible poet'. Marianne Moore saw him as 'a master of the anonymous'. Eliot recoiled from the idea of a biography because he did not want his literary work to be read as a coded commentary on events in his life. He was right to fear the worst. His first marriage is the subject of a play and a film. Speculation abounds about his sexuality in his early years. And what are we to make of his racial attitudes?

But what are we to make of his *poems*? His description of the creative process relates most pertinently to the early work. He says 'the emotion of art is impersonal'. The writer should experience 'a continual surrender of himself as he is at the moment to something which is more valuable. The progress of an artist is a continual self-sacrifice, a continual extinction of personality.' Such language borders, intentionally, on the religious and mystical.

Thomas Stearns Eliot was born in St Louis, Missouri, the seventh child of a company secretary who ultimately became chairman of the Hydraulic Press Brick Company, and a mother who was deeply cultured and wrote poems. The family was Unitarian in faith, believing in human perfectibility and distrusting ritual. Piety without sacrament, a smiling moral severity, and a settled materialism gave the young Eliot much against which to rebel, and he did so as Henry James had done before him, by choosing an exile in which he believed he could become himself.

He studied at Smith Academy in St Louis, and attended Harvard College between 1906 and 1910. Boston and Cambridge, Massachusetts, his first exile as it were, left a deeper impression on his early poems than St Louis had done. Eliot visited France in 1910, attending lectures at the Sorbonne, and returned to Harvard to pursue his doctorate on European and Indian philosophy in 1911. In 1914 he travelled to Marburg to pursue his studies, but with the First World War he turned up in England, gravitating to Merton College, Oxford, where he continued working on his doctoral thesis on the philosophy of F.H. Bradley. In 1915 he left university and married for the first time. He tried his hand at teaching in a junior school in London, then took a job at Lloyds Bank. He became a close friend of Ezra Pound. Though he spent his adult life in England, he regarded himself as an American poet.

In 1917 Eliot took over the editorship of the *Egoist* from Richard Aldington and in 1922 he founded his most influential magazine, *Criterion*, which established a standard of critical and creative writing. His years as a magazine editor coincided with his early success as a poet. In 1917 *Prufrock and Other Poems* appeared, and *Poems* (1920), *The Waste Land* (1922) and *The Hollow Men* (1925) seemed to change English poetry for good. Eliot became at first the most controversial, and then the most respected avant garde writer of his day. In 1927 he became a British subject and joined the Church of England. *Ash Wednesday* (1930), the first substantial production of the English Eliot, and the dramatic fragments *Sweeney Agonistes* (published in book form in 1932) have only latterly attracted the attention they merit. In 1944 his last major poetic work, *Four Quartets*, was published (*Burnt Norton*, 1935; *East Coker*, 1940; *The Dry Salvages*, 1941; *Little Gidding*, 1942). After that, most of his flagging poetic energies were directed to dramatic verse.

Eliot received many honours, including the Nobel Prize and the Order of Merit and was canonized as 'the poet of the century'.

La Figlia Che Piange

O quam te memorem virgo…

Stand on the highest pavement of the stair—
Lean on a garden urn—
Weave, weave the sunlight in your hair—
Clasp your flowers to you with a pained surprise—
Fling them to the ground and turn
With a fugitive resentment in your eyes:
But weave, weave the sunlight in your hair.

So I would have had him leave,
So I would have had her stand and grieve,
So he would have left
As the soul leaves the body torn and bruised,
As the mind deserts the body it has used.
I should find
Some way incomparably light and deft,
Some way we both should understand,
Simple and faithless as a smile and shake of the hand.

She turned away, but with the autumn weather
Compelled my imagination many days,
Many days and many hours:
Her hair over her arms and her arms full of flowers.
And I wonder how they should have been together!
I should have lost a gesture and a pose.
Sometimes these cogitations still amaze
The troubled midnight and the noon's repose.

The Love Song of J. Alfred Prufrock

S'io credessi che mia risposta fosse
a persona che mai tornasse al mondo,
questa fiamma staria senza più scosse.
Ma per ciò che giammai di questo fondo
non tornò vivo alcun, s'i'odo il vero,
senza tema d'infamia ti rispondo.

Let us go then, you and I,
When the evening is spread out against the sky
Like a patient etherised upon a table;
Let us go, through certain half-deserted streets,
The muttering retreats
Of restless nights in one-night cheap hotels
And sawdust restaurants with oyster-shells:

Streets that follow like a tedious argument
Of insidious intent
To lead you to an overwhelming question ...
Oh, do not ask, 'What is it?'
Let us go and make our visit.

In the room the women come and go
Talking of Michelangelo.

The yellow fog that rubs its back upon the window-panes,
The yellow smoke that rubs its muzzle on the window-panes
Licked its tongue into the corners of the evening,
Lingered upon the pools that stand in drains,
Let fall upon its back the soot that falls from chimneys,
Slipped by the terrace, made a sudden leap,
And seeing that it was a soft October night,
Curled once about the house, and fell asleep.

And indeed there will be time
For the yellow smoke that slides along the street
Rubbing its back upon the window-panes;
There will be time, there will be time
To prepare a face to meet the faces that you meet;
There will be time to murder and create,
And time for all the works and days of hands
That lift and drop a question on your plate;
Time for you and time for me,
And time yet for a hundred indecisions,
And for a hundred visions and revisions,
Before the taking of a toast and tea.

In the room the women come and go
Talking of Michelangelo.

And indeed there will be time
To wonder, 'Do I dare?' and, 'Do I dare?'
Time to turn back and descend the stair,
With a bald spot in the middle of my hair—
(They will say: 'How his hair is growing thin!')
My morning coat, my collar mounting firmly to the chin,
My necktie rich and modest, but asserted by a simple pin—
(They will say: 'But how his arms and legs are thin!')
Do I dare
Disturb the universe?
In a minute there is time
For decisions and revisions which a minute will reverse.

For I have known them all already, known them all—
Have known the evenings, mornings, afternoons,
I have measured out my life with coffee spoons;

> Have known the evenings, mornings, afternoons, I have measured out my life with coffee spoons

I know the voices dying with a dying fall
Beneath the music from a farther room.
　　So how should I presume?

　　And I have known the eyes already, known them all—
The eyes that fix you in a formulated phrase,
And when I am formulated, sprawling on a pin,
When I am pinned and wriggling on the wall,
Then how should I begin
To spit out all the butt-ends of my days and ways?
　　And how should I presume?

　　And I have known the arms already, known them all—
Arms that are braceleted and white and bare
(But in the lamplight, downed with light brown hair!)
Is it perfume from a dress
That makes me so digress?
Arms that lie along a table, or wrap about a shawl.
　　And should I then presume?
　　And how should I begin?
. . . . .

　　Shall I say, I have gone at dusk through narrow streets
And watched the smoke that rises from the pipes
Of lonely men in shirt-sleeves, leaning out of windows? . . .

I should have been a pair of ragged claws
Scuttling across the floors of silent seas.
. . . . .

　　And the afternoon, the evening, sleeps so peacefully!
Smoothed by long fingers,
Asleep . . . tired . . . or it malingers,
Stretched on the floor, here beside you and me.
Should I, after tea and cakes and ices,
Have the strength to force the moment to its crisis?
But though I have wept and fasted, wept and prayed,
Though I have seen my head (grown slightly bald) brought in upon a platter,
I am no prophet—and here's no great matter;
I have seen the moment of my greatness flicker,
And I have seen the eternal Footman hold my coat, and snicker,
And in short, I was afraid.

　　And would it have been worth it, after all,
After the cups, the marmalade, the tea,
Among the porcelain, among some talk of you and me,
Would it have been worth while,
To have bitten off the matter with a smile,
To have squeezed the universe into a ball

*I should have
been a pair
of ragged
claws
Scuttling
across the
floors of
silent seas.*

To roll it towards some overwhelming question,
To say: 'I am Lazarus, come from the dead,
Come back to tell you all, I shall tell you all'—
If one, settling a pillow by her head,
    Should say: 'That is not what I meant at all.
    That is not it, at all.'

    And would it have been worth it, after all,
Would it have been worth while,
After the sunsets and the dooryards and the sprinkled streets,
After the novels, after the teacups, after the skirts that trail along the floor—
And this, and so much more?—
It is impossible to say just what I mean!
But as if a magic lantern threw the nerves in patterns on a screen:
Would it have been worth while
If one, settling a pillow or throwing off a shawl,
And turning toward the window, should say:
    'That is not it at all,
    That is not what I meant, at all.'
. . . . .

    No! I am not Prince Hamlet, nor was meant to be;
Am an attendant lord, one that will do
To swell a progress, start a scene or two,
Advise the prince; no doubt, an easy tool,
Deferential, glad to be of use,
Politic, cautious, and meticulous;
Full of high sentence, but a bit obtuse;
At times, indeed, almost ridiculous—
Almost, at times, the Fool.

    I grow old . . . I grow old . . .
I shall wear the bottoms of my trousers rolled.

    Shall I part my hair behind? Do I dare to eat a peach?
I shall wear white flannel trousers, and walk upon the beach.
I have heard the mermaids singing, each to each.

I do not think that they will sing to me.

I have seen them riding seaward on the waves
Combing the white hair of the waves blown back
When the wind blows the water white and black.

We have lingered in the chambers of the sea
By sea-girls wreathed with seaweed red and brown
Till human voices wake us, and we drown.

No! I am not Prince Hamlet, nor was meant to be

Hugh
MacDiarmid

(1892–1978)

The Innumerable Christ

Light and Shadow

Crystals Like Blood

At My Father's Grave

The man whose ambition was to reinvent Scottish poetry began by reinventing himself. In 1922 Christopher Murray Grieve, at the age of 30, became the ineradicable Hugh MacDiarmid, his 'nom de plume (et de guerre)'. When he died 56 years later he had redrawn the map of Scottish poetry, affected the configuration of English literature and become the greatest Scottish poet since Burns.

Distressed at Scotland's willing cultural submission to England and its ignorance of its distinctive heritage, he made it his mission to revitalize the Scottish imagination. This involved re-inventing a Scottish language for poetry, as well as adapting Modernist techniques to specifically Scottish ends. Seamus Heaney noted: 'He prepared the ground for a Scottish literature that would be self-critical and experimental in relation to its own inherited forms and idioms, but one that would also be stimulated by developments elsewhere in world literature.' Because many of his best poems are in a Scottish language rooted in the vernacular of the Borders and Scottish Lowlands (Lallans), not standard English, he seems at first linguistically difficult. The difficulty as the work develops is less in the language, to which readers can soon adjust with the aid of a glossary, but in the huge lexicon he exploits in English and Lallans. His best verse is supple and various. His worst is not. A vast curate's egg: 'My job, as I see it, has never been to lay a tit's egg, but to erupt like a volcano, emitting not only flame, but a lot of rubbish.' He adhered to doubtful political causes of right and left, coming to rest upon a Marxism disfigured by an unalloyed respect for Stalin.

He was born and raised in Langholm, Dumfriesshire. He went to Edinburgh and began teacher's training but changed his mind and took up a career in journalism instead. He worked for the Fabian Research Department and contributed to A.R. Orage's *The New Age*. During the First World War he served in the Royal Artillery Medical Corps. He was a Scottish Nationalist and a Communist, expelled by the Nationalists for his membership of the Communist Party, and vice versa.

Poverty and a breakdown in health followed his second marriage and he withdrew (1933–41) to a croft on Whalsay in the Shetlands. During the Second World War he worked as an engineer on the Clyde and eventually settled in Biggar, Lanarkshire, where he lived until his death. The experiences he gathered in his alternately retiring and hectically active life, and the breadth of his reading, make him an encyclopaedically informed writer like Pound and Joyce, though his knowledge was less well organized than theirs, its structures less sustaining of the weight he put upon them.

His greatest poem – one of the great Modernist poems – is *A Drunk Man Looks at the Thistle* (1925). Unfortunately it cannot be excerpted for representation here, but many of its qualities are present in the shorter poems chosen. The speaker is resolutely Scottish, highly literate and very drunk. As he tumbles into a half-dream stupor beside the thistle in the moonlight, a flood of thoughts, jostling for precedence, flows out. The language is supple in its abrupt changes of tone and mood, sometimes within a single stanza or a single line. T.S. Eliot, no stranger to constructing a home in an alien culture, wrote: 'It will eventually be admitted that he has done … more for English poetry by committing some of his finest verse to Scots, than if he had elected to write exclusively in the Southern dialect.' In serving Scotland best, he served English literature as well.

The Innumerable Christ

Wha kens on whatna Bethlehems
Earth twinkles like a star the nicht,
An' whatna shepherds lift their heids
    In its unearthly licht?

'Yont a' the stars oor een can see
An' farther than their lichts can fly,
I' mony an unco warl' the nicht
    The fatefu' bairnies cry.

I' mony an unco warl' the nicht
The lift gaes black as pitch at noon,
An' sideways on their chests the heids
    O' endless Christs roll doon.

An' when the earth's as cauld's the mune
An' a' its folk are lang syne deid,
On coontless stars the babe maun cry
    An' the Crucified maun bleed.

> On coontless stars the
> babe maun cry

Light and Shadow

Like memories of what cannot be
Within the reign of memory...
That shake our mortal frames to dust

          Shelley

On every thought I have the countless shadows fall
Of other thoughts as valid that I cannot have;
Cross-lights of errors, too, impossible to me,
Yet somehow truer than all these thoughts, being with more power aglow.

May I never lose these shadowy glimpses of unknown thoughts
That modify and minify my own, and never fail
To keep some shining sense of the way all thoughts at last
Before life's dawning meaning like the stars at sunrise pale.

Crystals Like Blood

I remember how, long ago, I found
Crystals like blood in a broken stone.

I picked up a broken chunk of bed-rock
And turned it this way and that,
It was heavier than one would have expected
From its size. One face was caked
With brown limestone. But the rest
Was a hard greenish-grey quartz-like stone
Faintly dappled with darker shadows,
And in this quartz ran veins and beads
Of bright magenta.

And I remember how later on I saw
How mercury is extracted from cinnabar
– The double ring of piledrivers
Like the multiple legs of a fantastically symmetrical spider
Rising and falling with monotonous precision,
Marching round in an endless circle
And pounding up and down with a tireless, thunderous force,
While, beyond, another conveyor drew the crumbled ore
From the bottom and raised it to an opening high
In the side of a gigantic grey-white kiln.

So I remember how mercury is got
When I contrast my living memory of you
And your dear body rotting here in the clay
– And feel once again released in me
The bright torrents of felicity, naturalness, and faith
My treadmill memory draws from you yet.

At My Father's Grave

The sunlicht still on me, you row'd in clood,
We look upon each ither noo like hills
Across a valley. I'm nae mair your son.
It is my mind, nae son o' yours, that looks,
And the great darkness o' your death comes up
And equals it across the way.
A livin' man upon a deid man thinks
And ony sma'er thocht's impossible.

Edna
St. Vincent
Millay (1892–1950)

Time does not bring relief; you all have lied …

Recuerdo

Wild Swans

The Fawn

Born in Rockland, Maine, Edna St. Vincent Millay, the eldest of three daughters, was encouraged by her mother to explore the worlds of music and poetry. When she was 20 her work began to be recognized, especially the celebrated extended poem 'Renascence', a spiritual vision cast in lucid octosyllabic couplets; and thanks to a patron she was able to attend Vassar College. She moved to Greenwich Village in 1917 and made her living as an actress, playwright, satirist and freelance, continuing to compose poetry. Here she explored her sexual ambivalences, and here too she began her heavy drinking. As a correspondent, she was sent to Europe by *Vanity Fair* in 1921–2. By then her second book of poems had given her a wry reputation: she was becoming a poet to take seriously, a master of traditional forms whose originality was tonal and intellectual. Hers was the voice of the 'New Woman', speaking with unabashed frankness about love and other themes. In subsequent collections, the posed ironies and effects that coloured her writing diminished and an altogether less playful, more engaged lyrical voice emerged. She became the outstanding sonnet-writer of the twentieth century.

She married in 1923, the same year in which she was awarded the Pulitzer Prize for poetry, the first woman to receive it, and she travelled, went on reading tours and firmed up her audience across the United States. From 1925 her husband settled her at Steepletop in Austerlitz, New York. He wanted to give her freedom to engage uninterruptedly with her muse, and this he did; but she engaged to a degree in public controversies, most notably in her poems attempting to stay the execution of Sacco and Vanzetti in 1927; and later, as her reputation declined, she turned her hand to other kinds of work, including anti-fascist writing, remote from her earlier poetic concerns.

Setting Millay among the Modernists makes her seem a curiously old-fashioned, romantic spirit; she accepts and exploits traditional means and is not minded to disrupt or discard them; she writes directly about feelings, even awkward feelings, and the poems are always accessible. She has an old-fashioned reverence for poetic beauty and is not ashamed to devote herself to its pursuit. Her sense of life's ironies is acute, especially those treacherous ironies of love and a relationship developing and dying in time. She is not embarrassed by the exclamation mark – the vocative, the unabashed declaration. She does not question her tools, being keen instead on perfecting them. She is, in free verse as in metre, a consummate sound artist; there is no evidence, however, that she was brushed more than lightly by the wings of Modernism. She contributed to the development of a modern prosody, but the development of Modernist forms was of little interest to her.

The conventions with which her verse does battle were social, not poetic: she rejected the roles that had been devised for women, and other roles that demanded conformity and punished independence. Beyond roles there were the social and spiritual rules that seemed to underpin them and that she found sometimes intractable, sometimes arbitrary. Her sense of love, however, remained true to the young loves she had had. In her protected seclusion at Steepletop, she was able to revisit earlier intensities as they receded in time. Initially, this produced only elegies and wan re-creations of those earlier moments, but later this developed into resigned and eloquent philosophical and nature poetry.

Time does not bring relief; you all have lied...

Time does not bring relief; you all have lied
Who told me time would ease me of my pain!
I miss him in the weeping of the rain;
I want him at the shrinking of the tide;
The old snows melt from every mountain-side,
And last year's leaves are smoke in every lane;
But last year's bitter loving must remain
Heaped on my heart, and my old thoughts abide.
There are a hundred places where I fear
To go,—so with his memory they brim.
And entering with relief some quiet place
Where never fell his foot or shone his face
I say, 'There is no memory of him here!'
And so stand stricken, so remembering him.

I miss him in the weeping of the rain

Recuerdo

We were very tired, we were very merry—
We had gone back and forth all night on the ferry.
It was bare and bright, and smelled like a stable—
But we looked into a fire, we leaned across a table,
We lay on a hill-top underneath the moon;
And the whistles kept blowing, and the dawn came soon.

We were very tired, we were very merry—
We had gone back and forth all night on the ferry;
And you ate an apple, and I ate a pear,
From a dozen of each we had bought somewhere;
And the sky went wan, and the wind came cold,
And the sun rose dripping, a bucketful of gold.

We were very tired, we were very merry,
We had gone back and forth all night on the ferry.
We hailed, 'Good morrow, mother!' to a shawl-covered head,
And bought a morning paper, which neither of us read;
And she wept, 'God bless you!' for the apples and pears,
And we gave her all our money but our subway fares.

Wild Swans

I looked in my heart while the wild swans went over.
And what did I see I had not seen before?
Only a question less or a question more;
Nothing to match the flight of wild birds flying.
Tiresome heart, forever living and dying,
House without air, I leave you and lock your door.
Wild swans, come over the town, come over
The town again, trailing your legs and crying!

Was it alarm, or was it the wind
of my fear lest he depart

The Fawn

There it was I saw what I shall never forget
And never retrieve.
Monstrous and beautiful to human eyes, hard to believe,
He lay, yet there he lay,
Asleep on the moss, his head on his polished cleft small ebony hooves,
The child of the doe, the dappled child of the deer.

Surely his mother had never said, 'Lie here
Till I return,' so spotty and plain to see
On the green moss lay he.
His eyes had opened; he considered me.

I would have given more than I care to say
To thrifty ears, might I have had him for my friend
One moment only of that forest day:

Might I have had the acceptance, not the love
Of those clear eyes;
Might I have been for him in the bough above
Or the root beneath his forest bed,
A part of the forest, seen without surprise.

Was it alarm, or was it the wind of my fear lest he depart
That jerked him to his jointy knees,
And sent him crashing off, leaping and stumbling
On his new legs, between the stems of the white trees?

Wilfred
Owen
(1893–1918)

The Parable of the Old Man and the Young

Futility

Strange Meeting

The most celebrated English-language war poet, Wilfred Owen was born in Oswestry, Shropshire, where he spent a happy childhood. At the age of ten he visited Broxton by the Hill and there, he declared in arch retrospect, 'first I felt my boyhood fill / With uncontainable movements; there was born / My poethood.'

He was educated at the Birkenhead Institute, Shrewsbury Technical College, and London University. The teacher and First World War poet Edmund Blunden recalls that he tended to choose his friends for what he could get from them – intellectual stimulus, principally. His idol was Keats, whom he celebrated and to whose shrines he made pilgrimage. His devotion to the beautiful is often expressed in a Keatsian spirit; his imagination was steeped in elegiac Romanticism and even to the most literal scenes a kind of literary varnish is applied.

In 1913 he wrote half-seriously of his plan to publish 'Minor Poems – in Minor Keys – By a Minor'. The earliest writings are little more. Sharp, sensuous passages do occur, but set in a hectic tide of assonance and alliteration. He was, like most young poets, too fond of adjectives and adverbs which steal the limelight from perfectly adequate nouns and verbs. He spent two years teaching English in France (1913–15) and made some literary friendships.

In 1915 Owen enlisted in the Artists' Rifles and went to war. Under intolerable stress he was invalided out in 1917 and convalesced near Edinburgh, where he was befriended by the already established and dissident poet Siegfried Sassoon. They discussed poetry and other topics and Owen's admiration knew no bounds. He calls Sassoon his 'Keats + Christ + Elijah + my Colonel + my father-confessor + Amenophus IV, in profile'. Sassoon talked about the war and pacifism. Owen became less a poet than a war poet, his mission to dramatize for those at home the situation of the soldier in the trenches, how fear of death and the presence of suffering numbed men or drove them mad. A sense of duty coupled with a gnawing masochism sent him back to the Front, and after writing more poems and enduring the worst of the last campaign, he was awarded the Military Cross, and was killed the week before the armistice.

'The new material, if it could be presented at all, needed a profound linguistic invention,' C.H. Sisson writes. Owen experimented with metre and rhyme, but his experiments developed or refined common poetic techniques, they did not break new ground. His approach is not formally radical, his blend of irony and pity not new – we have it in Hardy, Housman, Kipling and earlier. But his subject matter is new, as is his fascination with the detail of physical suffering.

At heart Owen is less a realist than an idealist. He is drawn to the ugly and sordid because he is attracted to the beautiful. When he realized how poignantly the hideous could be conveyed in terms previously reserved for the beautiful, his work developed in distinctiveness. Owen can express intense love and describe intense physical agony in the same forms. The maimed man and the pastoral landscape are given similar rhythms. In the famous 'Preface' to the poems – rough notes, not a finished essay – he asserts: 'This book is not about heroes. English poetry is not yet fit to speak of them,' forgetting the tradition in which he writes. 'Above all,' he continues, 'I am not concerned with Poetry.' In fact, he is profoundly concerned with it and knows how he would like to add to its resources.

The Parable of the Old Man and the Young

So Abram rose, and clave the wood, and went,
And took the fire with him, and a knife.
And as they sojourned both of them together,
Isaac the first-born spake and said, My Father,
Behold the preparations, fire and iron,
But where the lamb, for this burnt-offering?
Then Abram bound the youth with belts and straps,
And builded parapets and trenches there,
And stretchèd forth the knife to slay his son.
When lo! an Angel called him out of heaven,
Saying, Lay not thy hand upon the lad,
Neither do anything to him, thy son.
Behold! Caught in a thicket by its horns,
A Ram. Offer the Ram of Pride instead.

But the old man would not so, but slew his son,
And half the seed of Europe, one by one.

Then Abram bound the
youth with belts and straps

Futility

Move him into the sun–
Gently its touch awoke him once,
At home, whispering of fields half-sown.
Always it woke him, even in France,
Until this morning and this snow.
If anything might rouse him now
The kind old sun will know.

Think how it wakes the seeds–
Woke once the clays of a cold star.
Are limbs, so dear achieved, are sides
Full-nerved, still warm, too hard to stir?
Was it for this the clay grew tall?
–O what made fatuous sunbeams toil
To break earth's sleep at all?

Strange Meeting

It seemed that out of battle I escaped
Down some profound dull tunnel, long since scooped
Through granites which titanic wars had groined.

Yet also there encumbered sleepers groaned,
Too fast in thought or death to be bestirred.
Then, as I probed them, one sprang up, and stared
With piteous recognition in fixed eyes,
Lifting distressful hands, as if to bless.
And by his smile, I knew that sullen hall,–
By his dead smile I knew we stood in Hell.

With a thousand pains that vision's face was grained;
Yet no blood reached there from the upper ground,
And no guns thumped, or down the flues made moan.
'Strange friend,' I said, 'here is no cause to mourn.'
'None,' said that other, 'save the undone years,
The hopelessness. Whatever hope is yours,
Was my life also; I went hunting wild
After the wildest beauty in the world,
Which lies not calm in eyes, or braided hair,
But mocks the steady running of the hour,
And if it grieves, grieves richlier than here.
For by my glee might many men have laughed,
And of my weeping something had been left,
Which must die now. I mean the truth untold,
The pity of war, the pity war distilled.
Now men will go content with what we spoiled,
Or, discontent, boil bloody, and be spilled.
They will be swift with swiftness of the tigress.
None will break ranks, though nations trek from progress.
Courage was mine, and I had mystery,
Wisdom was mine, and I had mastery:
To miss the march of this retreating world
Into vain citadels that are not walled.
Then, when much blood had clogged their chariot-wheels,
I would go up and wash them from sweet wells,
Even with truths that lie too deep for taint.
I would have poured my spirit without stint
But not through wounds; not on the cess of war.
Foreheads of men have bled where no wounds were.

'I am the enemy you killed, my friend.
I knew you in this dark: for so you frowned
Yesterday through me as you jabbed and killed.
I parried; but my hands were loath and cold.
Let us sleep now…'

The pity of war, the pity war distilled.

E.E.
Cummings

(1894–1962)

in Just

what if a much of a which of a wind

pity this busy monster, manunkind

Reading his name as he wrote it, without capital letters, one is tempted to ask whether Edward Estlin Cummings is modest or arrogant. A third possibility: he is political. The re-inventers of poetry sometimes re-invented the adversary. Cummings came up, as Pound and Jeffers and Owen differently had done, with a corrupt and corrupting political adversary, 'manunkind', the collective 'busy monster' that consumes, betrays and destroys the joyfully anarchic individual. At the time of the Hungarian uprising (1957) the poet wrote:

> so rah-rah-rah democracy
> let's all be as thankful as hell
> and bury the statue of liberty
> (because it begins to smell)

The lyrical Cummings remains popular but it is worth remembering that the satirical Cummings retains his force, travelling more confidently through time than amorous-linguistic whimsy and the sentimentality it can mask.

Edward Estlin Cummings was born in Cambridge, Massachusetts. His father, an English teacher at Harvard, dropped out to become a Unitarian minister in Boston, eventually at the famous Old South Church. Through his father he was rooted in New England Transcendentalism. The boy took a BA and an MA at Harvard, served in the First World War as an ambulance driver and soldier, and spent some months in a French detention camp on a trumped up charge (the censor had not liked his letters home), which gave him material for his American-Kafkaesque memoir-novel *The Enormous Room* (1922). His first volume of poems, *Tulips and Chimneys* (1923) experimented with letters whilst using conventional forms.

Later came experiments with type, learned perhaps from Apollinaire, an attempt to bring into the text the qualities of vocalization he required, by gaps, spaces, drop margins; and to indicate how many other words a word contains by laying it out in revealing ways. The mimesis is aural and visual at once, and our whole attention is required less for the flow of language than the dance and counter-dance of words. The poetry is, in a very constricted sense, on the page as deliberate pattern.

Introducing *Poems 1924–1954* he wrote, 'Life, for eternal us, is now'. The 'eternal us' are the poet and his select readers, not 'mostpeople' who don't like poetry and, in Cummings's view, don't have reckonable lives. The complicity into which he invites us, the arrogance we are required to accept and applaud, come to seem now anti-human, and inconsequential.

Cummings divided his life between Paris and Greenwich Village, and later between the Village and his New Hampshire farm. He died in 1962. Never happy in a single form, he more than dabbled in painting and drawing, he based a satirical ballet on *Uncle Tom's Cabin*, wrote plays and a travel diary about his trip to the Soviet Union, *Eimi* (1933), because he was fascinated with the human experiment of Communism. Poems were his primary activity, but set against those of other Modernists, his are soft-centred. Cummings is a dialect poet in the way he releases sense from words that seem familiar and a little weary. His belief in the Individual, the anarchic 'I' in tension or conflict with the world and its institutions, issues in inventive distortions – but not in much more than a derangement of surfaces, hardly a radical vision, a reinvention of form. Yet of all the moderns it is Cummings who found his way most readily into the hearts of general readers.

in Just

in Just-
spring   when the world is mud-
luscious the little
lame balloonman

whistles   far   and wee

and eddieandbill come
running from marbles and
piracies and it's
spring

when the world is puddle-wonderful

the queer
old balloonman whistles
far   and   wee
and bettyandisbel come dancing

from hop-scotch and jump-rope and

it's
spring
and
        the

                goat-footed

balloonMan   whistles
far
and
wee

*when the world is
puddle-wonderful*

what if a much of a which of a wind

what if a much of a which of a wind
gives the truth to summer's lie;
bloodies with dizzying leaves the sun
and yanks immortal stars awry?
Blow king to beggar and queen to seem
(blow friend to fiend:blow space to time)
—when skies are hanged and oceans drowned,
the single secret will still be man

what if a keen of a lean wind flays
screaming hills with sleet and snow:
strangles valleys by ropes of thing

and stifles forests in white ago?
Blow hope to terror;blow seeing to blind
(blow pity to envy and soul to mind)
—whose hearts are mountains,roots are trees,
it's they shall cry hello to the spring

what if a dawn of a doom of a dream
bites this universe in two,
peels forever out of his grave
and sprinkles nowhere with me and you?
Blow soon to never and never to twice
(blow life to isn't:blow death to was)
—all nothing's only our hugest home;
the most who die,the more we live

pity this busy monster, manunkind

pity this busy monster,manunkind,

not. Progress is a comfortable disease:
your victim(death and life safely beyond)

plays with the bigness of his littleness
—electrons deify one razorblade
into a mountainrange;lenses extend

unwish through curving wherewhen till unwish
returns on its unself.
               A world of made
is not a world of born—pity poor flesh

and trees,poor stars and stones,but never this
fine specimen of hypermagical

ultraomnipotence. We doctors know

a hopeless case if—listen: there's a hell
of a good universe next door;let's go

unwish through
curving wherewhen
till unwish

Robert
Graves
(1895–1985)

The Cool Web

In Broken Images

To Juan at the Winter Solstice

Robert Graves declared, 'experimental work, as such, has no future. Last year's experimental poem is as out of date as last year's hat and there must come a time, perhaps not very many years hence, when there will be a nostalgic reaction from futurism to some sort of traditionalism, and in the end, back will come the Miltonic sonnet, the Spenserian stanza and the mock-heroic epic in the style of Pope.' He kicked insistently against what he took to be the merely new: 'I should define a good poem as one that makes complete sense; and says all it has to say memorably and economically; and has been written for no other than poetic reasons.'

He proposes an ancient mission for poetry, an earnest and delighted engagement with language. His experience and survival of the First World War darken his imagination. War hangs over many of the poems. He left England, establishing an 'old habit of non-residence', prompted by a love of the Mediterranean – he settled in Majorca – and by a rejection of industry and its dehumanizing technologies, the desecration of native landscape, a modern devaluing of relationships and standards. Retrospective radical rather than reactionary, he longs for an unregainable world, one that went with the war.

Robert Ranke Graves was born in London, son of an Irish poet, songwriter and folklorist. He grew up in a highly literate household. Before he attended Charterhouse School he was already writing. He went to St John's College, Oxford, where the war interrupted his education. He joined the British Expeditionary Force and served in France, was wounded and suffered from shell-shock. He was reported dead; indeed, he read his own obituary in *The Times* before his twenty-first birthday.

In late 1926 Graves's life abruptly altered. He had been corresponding with the American poet Laura Riding and invited her to join him and his wife on a journey to Egypt. She arrived and took him in hand, as a poet and as a person. Through her severe ministrations he at last moved clear of the traumatized war years. What he called 'the strong pulling of her bladed mind' left no area of his concerns untouched and untransformed. With her he prepared *A Survey of Modernist Poetry* (1927): 'the reader should enter the life of the poem and submit himself to its conditions to know it as it really is.' Adopting the impersonality – or neutrality – that the poet has adopted, a reader must accept before he can know.

The turbulent, often fruitful relationship with Laura Riding, and with the poets and artists who came to Majorca to be with this extraordinary pair, ended in 1939. With the Second World War they had to leave the island. In 1956 Graves returned and set up permanent residence there. His most provocative book of the post-Riding years, *The White Goddess* (1946), was a 'historical grammar of poetic myth'. His thesis is that poetry is written in thrall to the muse: the White Goddess. She is a figure defined in some of the poems, notably 'To Juan at the Winter Solstice' which celebrates her omnipresence and ineffable quality. Reviled by saints and sober men, she is the lady of extremes, vitality, imbalance: creative and destructive, she lives within and outside the individual, she burns off all but his capacity for love. She has no constant rules, she is 'Sister of the mirage and the echo'. Through her, Graves externalizes and mythologizes his own tensions. The myth expresses his extremely personal vision – constructed, not instinctive.

The Cool Web

Children are dumb to say how hot the day is,
How hot the scent is of the summer rose,
How dreadful the black wastes of evening sky,
How dreadful the tall soldiers drumming by.

But we have speech, to chill the angry day,
And speech, to dull the rose's cruel scent.
We spell away the overhanging night,
We spell away the soldiers and the fright.

There's a cool web of language winds us in,
Retreat from too much joy or too much fear:
We grow sea-green at last and coldly die
In brininess and volubility.

But if we let our tongues lose self-possession,
Throwing off language and its watery clasp
Before our death, instead of when death comes,
Facing the wide glare of the children's day,
Facing the rose, the dark sky and the drums,
We shall go mad no doubt and die that way.

*There's a
cool web of
language
winds us in,*

In Broken Images

He is quick, thinking in clear images;
I am slow, thinking in broken images.

He becomes dull, trusting to his clear images;
I become sharp, mistrusting my broken images.

Trusting his images, he assumes their relevance;
Mistrusting my images, I question their relevance.

Assuming their relevance, he assumes the fact;
Questioning their relevance, I question the fact.

When the fact fails him, he questions his senses;
When the fact fails me, I approve my senses.

He continues quick and dull in his clear images;
I continue slow and sharp in my broken images.

He in a new confusion of his understanding;
I in a new understanding of my confusion.

To Juan at the Winter Solstice

There is one story and one story only
That will prove worth your telling,
Whether as learned bard or gifted child;
To it all lines or lesser gauds belong
That startle with their shining
Such common stories as they stray into.

Is it of trees you tell, their months and virtues,
Or strange beasts that beset you,
Of birds that croak at you the Triple will?
Or of the Zodiac and how slow it turns
Below the Boreal Crown,
Prison to all true kings that ever reigned?

Water to water, ark again to ark,
From woman back to woman:
So each new victim treads unfalteringly
The never altered circuit of his fate,
Bringing twelve peers as witness
Both to his starry rise and starry fall.

Or is it of the Virgin's silver beauty,
All fish below the thighs?
She in her left hand bears a leafy quince;
When with her right hand she crooks a finger, smiling,
How may the King hold back?
Royally then he barters life for love.

Or of the undying snake from chaos hatched,
Whose coils contain the ocean,
Into whose chops with naked sword he springs,
Then in black water, tangled by the reeds,
Battles three days and nights,
To be spewed up beside her scalloped shore?

Much snow is falling, winds roar hollowly,
The owl hoots from the elder,
Fear in your heart cries to the loving-cup:
Sorrow to sorrow as the sparks fly upward.
The log groans and confesses:
There is one story and one story only.

Dwell on her graciousness, dwell on her smiling,
Do not forget what flowers
The great boar trampled down in ivy time.
Her brow was creamy as the crested wave,
Her sea-blue eyes were wild
But nothing promised that is not performed.

There is one
story and one
story only.

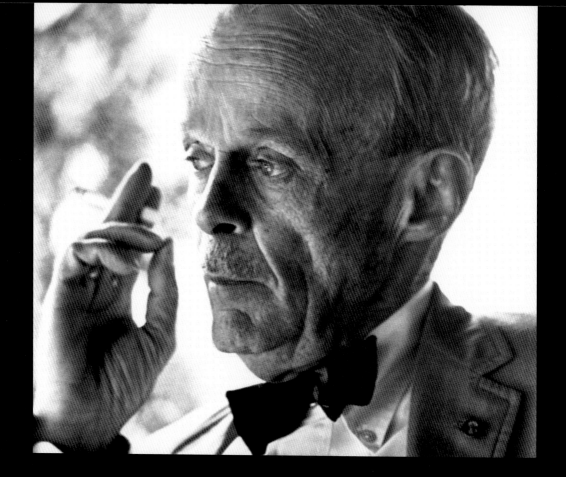

Allen **Tate**

(1899–1979)

Ode to the Confederate Dead

The Fugitives were an unusual group of American poets who defined a poetic route, kept to and extended it. They first promulgated it in the magazine *The Fugitive* which ran from 1922–25 (nineteen issues) and carried little but poetry, poetry, and poetry, with a brief editorial and a small review section. In 1928 *Fugitives: An Anthology of Verse* was published in New York and the movement was technically over, though its legacy persists.

Part of its dynamic was political. It was Southern, it issued in an agrarian ideology which can be seen as radical or terminally reactionary. It had certain chips on its shoulder: Chicago, New York and London were the literary centres, but Nashville, Tennessee, just wasn't on the map. It also had some fine poets and critics associated with it, in particular John Crowe Ransom and Allen Tate; and in Robert Penn Warren the most influential American critic-anthologist of his century. His anthology *Understanding Poetry*, edited with Cleanth Brooks, determined the taste of several generations of readers, establishing the 'New Criticism', devoted to close reading of texts along formal and a-historical lines.

'Fugitive' entailed dissent and flight from the disorder of the modern. Allen Tate (1899–1979), the youngster of the group, taken on board while still a student at Vanderbilt, was the firebrand. He defended *The Waste Land* against Ransom – he stood up to the master. He was the 'Easterner' among these men of the South (an 'Easterner' born in Kentucky), yet his 'Ode to the Confederate Dead', against the grain of which Robert Lowell later wrote 'For the Union Dead', is the great Southern poem of the first half of the century, magnificent in scope and in technical resource. It is no wonder that Lowell, disaffected with Boston, his family, his heritage and his church, sought out Tate when, a literal fugitive, he left Harvard. From Tate he learned that, 'A good poem had nothing to do with exalted feelings of being moved by the spirit': it was 'a piece of craftsmanship'. And that craftsmanship had to reveal itself *as* craftsmanship, not the art that conceals art. Tate was a fine satirist and a critic, but he regarded his main achievement to be an elaborate, elaborated, almost baroque metaphysical poetry, seemingly archaic at times, yet with a timeless clarity when it achieves its points of focus and definition.

Tate had a curious habit in his diction of using words in unexpected combinations that stripped them of their usual shades of meaning, of their implications and of the memory of their use in earlier poems. Context gave each word a single meaning. This disruption of conventional syntax, this new-minting of words, had an abiding impact on later poets, from Robert Lowell to Geoffrey Hill. Tate is a complex and serious poet, often obscure, always eloquent: a poet's poet. In his criticism there is awkward argumentativeness and rhetorical elevation, not like Eliot's secure patrician tone which makes us all patricians with him, but rather schoolmasterly, aimed a little above where his audience's heads are assumed to be.

Ode to the Confederate Dead

Row after row with strict impunity
The headstones yield their names to the element,
The wind whirrs without recollection;
In the riven troughs the splayed leaves
Pile up, of nature the casual sacrament
To the seasonal eternity of death;
Then driven by the fierce scrutiny
Of heaven to their election in the vast breath,
They sough the rumour of mortality.

Autumn is desolation in the plot
Of a thousand acres where these memories grow
From the inexhaustible bodies that are not
Dead, but feed the grass row after rich row.
Think of the autumns that have come and gone!—
Ambitious November with the humors of the year,
With a particular zeal for every slab,
Staining the uncomfortable angels that rot
On the slabs, a wing chipped here, an arm there:
The brute curiosity of an angel's stare
Turns you, like them, to stone,
Transforms the heaving air
Till plunged to a heavier world below
You shift your sea-space blindly
Heaving, turning like the blind crab.

       Dazed by the wind, only the wind
       The leaves flying, plunge

You know who have waited by the wall
The twilight certainty of an animal,
Those midnight restitutions of the blood
You know—the immitigable pines, the smoky frieze
Of the sky, the sudden call: you know the rage,
The cold pool left by the mounting flood,
Of muted Zeno and Parmenides.
You who have waited for the angry resolution
Of those desires that should be yours tomorrow,
You know the unimportant shrift of death
And praise the vision
And praise the arrogant circumstance
Of those who fall
Rank upon rank, hurried beyond decision—
Here by the sagging gate, stopped by the wall.

       Seeing, seeing only the leaves
       Flying, plunge and expire

Turn your eyes to the immoderate past,
Turn to the inscrutable infantry rising
Demons out of the earth they will not last.

From the
inexhaustible
bodies that
are not
Dead, but
feed the
grass row
after rich row.

Stonewall, Stonewall, and the sunken fields of hemp,
Shiloh, Antietam, Malvern Hill, Bull Run.
Lost in that orient of the thick-and-fast
You will curse the setting sun.

      Cursing only the leaves crying
      Like an old man in a storm

You hear the shout, the crazy hemlocks point
With troubled fingers to the silence which
Smothers you, a mummy, in time.
                    The hound bitch
Toothless and dying, in a musty cellar
Hears the wind only.
              Now that the salt of their blood
Stiffens the saltier oblivion of the sea,
Seals the malignant purity of the flood,
What shall we who count our days and bow
Our heads with a commemorial woe
In the ribboned coats of grim felicity,
What shall we say of the bones, unclean,
Whose verdurous anonymity will grow?
The ragged arms, the ragged heads and eyes
Lost in these acres of the insane green?
The gray lean spiders come, they come and go;
In a tangle of willows without light
The singular screech-owl's tight
Invisible lyric seeds the mind
With the furious murmur of their chivalry.

      We shall say only the leaves
      Flying, plunge and expire

We shall say only the leaves whispering
In the improbable mist of nightfall
That flies on multiple wing:
Night is the beginning and the end
And in between the ends of distraction
Waits mute speculation, the patient curse
That stones the eyes, or like the jaguar leaps
For his own image in a jungle pool, his victim.
What shall we say who have knowledge
Carried to the heart? Shall we take the act
To the grave? Shall we, more hopeful, set up the grave
In the house? The ravenous grave?

             Leave now
The shut gate and the decomposing wall:
The gentle serpent, green in the mulberry bush,
Riots with his tongue through the hush—
Sentinel of the grave who counts us all!

The gray
lean spiders
come,
they come
and go

Basil
Bunting
(1900–1985)

From Chomei at Toyama (1932)

Basil Bunting spent several years in Persia, on the edge of a real desert, yet the poetic landscapes he created are greener, often English – the England of his native Northumberland, with its history. Bunting was associated with the Objectivists but he could lend himself to that American movement, rooted in Pound and Williams, only in part. The rest of him was empirical, pragmatic; he trusted himself more than he trusted rules and programmes. He sat at Pound's feet, but he never merely imitated him.

Late in life he printed up a sheet entitled 'I SUGGEST', a positive version of Pound's 'A Few Don'ts': '1. Compose aloud: poetry is a sound.' Poetry 'lies dead on the page, until some voice brings it to life, just as music on the stave is no more than instruction to the player'. He regularly draws an analogy between poetry and music. 'The further poetry and music get from the dance and from each other, the less satisfactory they seem.' The points that follow are built on this governing principle. '2. Vary rhythm enough to stir the emotion you want but not so as to lose impetus. 3. Use spoken words and syntax. 4. Fear adjectives; they bleed nouns. Hate the passive. 5. Jettison ornament gaily but keep shape.'

He adds a Horatian injunction, 'Put your poem away till you forget it', then: '6. Cut out every word you dare. 7. Do it again a week later, and again.' His final advice is of a piece with Eliot's refusal to elucidate: 'Never explain – your reader is as smart as you.' 'Your reader' is not just any reader but the rare one with ears on his or her head. Readers of Bunting's work were rare indeed for much of his life. After decades of neglect, he was 'discovered'. *Briggflatts* (1966) and the *Collected Poems* (1968) made it impossible to overlook him any longer. By the time of his death in 1985 he was generally accepted as a major figure.

Born into a Quaker family, he was also born to Northumberland dialect whose inflections he retained in his poetry despite long exile. Quaker school encouraged his independence and his distrust of institution and hierarchy. He spent six months in prison as a conscientious objector to National Service in 1918, and the next year went to London to become a journalist. In 1923, when he met Pound in Paris, he sub-edited Ford Madox Ford's *Transatlantic Review*, then moved to Italy to work near Pound in Rapallo. There he met Yeats, who characterized him as 'one of Ezra's more savage disciples'.

In the Second World War Bunting joined the Air Force (it was a different sort of war from the First) and was sent to Persia. After the war he stayed on with the British Diplomatic Service as Vice-Consul in Isphahan, where he married a Persian wife in 1948. He left, only to return later as a journalist for *The Times*, but was expelled by Mossadeq. He returned to Northumberland and began to write once more, producing his best work, emerging into celebrity, in demand on the international reading circuit and honoured as the last Modernist, the one few had heard of before.

Unlike other Modernists, his work represents a break with tradition, not a reformulation of it. Those who insist on his debt to Pound tend to overlook a prior debt to Wordsworth, to Tudor and Elizabethan models, to Yeats, to the French Symbolists, and despite a settled personal aversion, to Eliot. His *Collected Poems*, even the later editions, constitute a concise *oeuvre*, but an essential one.

From Chomei at Toyama (1932)

(Kamo-no-Chomei, born at Kamo 1154, died at Toyama on Mount Hino, 24 June 1216)

Swirl sleeping in the waterfall!
On motionless pools scum appearing
             disappearing!

Eaves formal on the zenith,
lofty city Kyoto,
wealthy, without antiquities!

Housebreakers clamber about,
builders raising floor upon floor
at the corner sites, replacing
gardens by bungalows.

In the town where I was known
the young men stare at me.
A few faces I know remain.

Whence comes man at his birth? or where
does death lead him? Whom do you mourn?
Whose steps wake your delight?
Dewy hibiscus dries: though dew
outlast the petals. […]

[…] My grandmother left me a house
but I was always away
for my health and because I was alone there.
When I was thirty I couldn't stand it any longer,
I built a house to suit myself:
one bamboo room, you would have thought it a cartshed,
poor shelter from snow or wind.
It stood on the flood plain. And that quarter
is also flooded with gangsters.

One generation
I saddened myself with idealistic philosophies,
but before I was fifty
I perceived there was no time to lose,
left home and conversation.
Among the cloudy mountains of Ohara
spring and autumn, spring and autumn, spring and autumn,
emptier than ever.

The dew evaporates from my sixty years,
I have built my last house, or hovel,

I saddened
myself
with idealistic
philosophies

a hunter's bivouac, an old
silkworm's cocoon:
ten feet by ten, seven high: and I,
reckoning it a lodging not a dwelling,
omitted the usual foundation ceremony.

I have filled the frames with clay,
set hinges at the corners;
easy to take it down and carry it away
when I get bored with this place.
Two barrowloads of junk
and the cost of a man to shove the barrow,
no trouble at all.

Since I have trodden Hino mountain
noon has beaten through the awning
over my bamboo balcony, evening
shone on Amida.
I have shelved my books above the window,
lute and mandolin near at hand,
piled bracken and a little straw for bedding,
a smooth desk where the light falls, stove for bramblewood.
I have gathered stones, fitted
stones for a cistern, laid bamboo
pipes. No woodstack,
wood enough in the thicket.

Toyama, snug in the creepers!
Toyama, deep in the dense gully, open
westward whence the dead ride out of Eden
squatting on blue clouds of wistaria.
(Its scent drifts west to Amida.)

Summer? Cuckoo's *Follow, follow*—to
harvest Purgatory hill!
Fall? The nightgrasshopper will
shrill *Fickle life*!
Snow will thicken on the doorstep,
melt like a drift of sins.
No friend to break silence,
no one will be shocked if I neglect the rite.
There's a Lent of commandments kept
where there's no way to break them. [...]

Laura
Riding
(1901–1991)

A city seems ...
The World and I
The Troubles of a Book

Laura (Riding) Jackson, or Laura Riding née Reichenthal, was born in New York in 1901. At Cornell University she began to write poems, married a history instructor, and moved with him to the University of Louisville, Kentucky. Her 'lost' early poems were rediscovered and published in 1992, an amazing collection which shows how early, and how completely, she had conceived and mastered her distinctive manner. 'A city seems between us. It is only love,' is a fine example.

She became involved with the Fugitive Group, having submitted poems to their magazine. Allen Tate responded to her intelligence but stood in awe of her conviction, and the group itself stepped back from her. Robert Graves admired a poem of hers, they fell into correspondence, and he invited her to England. Much followed from that generative relationship.

'Truth', she declared, was her objective in life as in language. Poetry was to be the means of reaching it. For 20 years she tried to make it so. 'Her finest poems,' says Robert Nye, one of her most sympathetic editors, 'seem to me to be those in which she makes discovery as she writes, poems in which the heart's and mind's truth comes more as something learned than something taught.' 'The Trouble of a Book', 'Come, Words, Away', 'As Many Questions as Answers', 'Nor is it written that you may not grieve' and more than a score of other poems set this poet apart and above many reputations that loom larger.

After two decades' writing, she had said all that she could in verse, and it was not close enough to the kind of truth she wanted to tell. In 1939 she abandoned poetry, explaining her decision at length and amplifying her explanation in the years that followed. She abandoned Graves and returned to America where she devoted her remaining half century to *Rational Meaning: A New Foundation for the Definition of Words*, undertaken initially with Schuyler B. Jackson, whom she married in 1941 and with whom she lived until his death in 1968. Laura (Riding) Jackson, as she now styled herself, continued in her poetryless later years to insist on the truth-quest; also trying to establish, against dozens of readings and misreadings, the biographical and bibliographical truth of her relationship with Robert Graves.

Michael Roberts (1902–48), the anthologist, essayist and poet, summarized her stance: 'Poetry is the final residue of significance in language, freed from extrinsic decoration, superficial contemporaneity, and didactic bias.' She helped Roberts draft the introduction to the definitive anthology of its time, the *Faber Book of Modern Verse*, insisting there that 'the poetic use of language can cause discord as easily as it can cure it. A bad poem, a psychologically disordered poem, if it is technically effective may arouse uneasiness or nausea or anger in the reader.' The poet has actual power over readers and must work with care. She rejected the growing prejudice in favour of 'voice' in poetry, suggesting instead that the voice that matters is that of 'a man talking to men' rather than 'this particular man' talking to men. The eccentric individuation of her contemporaries repelled her: their writing put personality before language in a spirit of self-display, corrupting the mission of poetry.

A city seems …

A city seems between us. It is only love,
Love like a sorrow still
After a labor, after light.
The crowds are one.
Sleep is a single heart
Filling the old avenues we used to know
With miracles of dark and dread
We dare not go to meet
Save as our own dead stalking
Or as two dreams walking
One tread and terrible,
One cloak of longing in the cold,
Though we stand separate and wakeful
Measuring death in miles between us
Where a city seems and memories
Sleep like a populace.

One cloak
of longing in
the cold

The World and I

This is not exactly what I mean
Any more than the sun is the sun.
But how to mean more closely
If the sun shines but approximately?
What a world of awkwardness!
What hostile implements of sense!
Perhaps this is as close a meaning
As perhaps becomes such knowing.
Else I think the world and I
Must live together as strangers and die—
A sour love, each doubtful whether
Was ever a thing to love the other.
No, better for both to be nearly sure
Each of each—exactly where
Exactly I and exactly the world
Fail to meet by a moment, and a word.

What a world
of awkwardness!

The Troubles of a Book

The trouble of a book is first to be
No thoughts to nobody,
Then to lie as long unwritten
As it will lie unread,
Then to build word for word an author
And occupy his head
Until the head declares vacancy
To make full publication
Of running empty.

The trouble of a book is secondly
To keep awake and ready
And listening like an innkeeper,
Wishing, not wishing for a guest,
Torn between hope of no rest
And hope of rest.
Uncertainly the pages doze
And blink open to passing fingers
With landlord smile, then close.

The trouble of a book is thirdly
To speak its sermon, then look the other way,
Arouse commotion in the margin,
Where tongue meets the eye,
But claim no experience of panic,
No complicity in the outcry.
The ordeal of a book is to give no hint
Of ordeal, to be flat and witless
Of the upright sense of print.

The trouble of a book is chiefly
To be nothing but book outwardly;
To wear binding like binding,
Bury itself in book-death,
Yet to feel all but book;
To breathe live words, yet with the breath
Of letters; to address liveliness
In reading eyes, be answered with
Letters and bookishness.

To speak its
sermon,
then look the
other way

Langston
Hughes
(1902–1967)

The Negro Speaks of Rivers

My People

Cross

I too

During the Harlem Renaissance, which centred on the vital musical culture, the outstanding novelists wrote some powerful novels that included dialogue in their own idiom, though the narrative was generally conventional. What Langston Hughes set out to do was to use the cadences, natural metaphors and dialect elements as primary material for his verse and prose and for his famous Jesse B. Semple letters. 'Speak that I may see thee,' said Ben Jonson. In Hughes's work a whole community is made visible through its distinctive speech.

Hughes was born in Joplin, Missouri, and grew up with his maternal grandmother, his parents being separated. But he stayed some of the time with his mother in Detroit and Cleveland. There he completed high school and began writing verse, encouraged by her. His father, weary of racial prejudice, had gone to live in Mexico, and the budding poet visited him there. Theirs was not a happy relationship. Hughes attended Columbia University for one year, dropped out, travelled and did a variety of jobs: merchant seaman, nightclub work in Paris, busboy in Washington. He wrote and wrote and in 1925 some of his poems were published in *The New Negro*. The editor Carl Van Vechten took up his cause and arranged for his first book to be published. *The Weary Blues* appeared in 1926. Other white champions of the Harlem Renaissance also took an interest in him; he finished his studies at Lincoln University and settled in New York. By 1930 he was able to live from his writings and was dubbed 'the bard of Harlem'.

He became a public figure, helping to develop black theatre in Los Angeles, Chicago and in Harlem. He published in many genres, but poetry was his chief vocation, even though it did not butter bread the way his prose writings did. His work developed principally two modes: one drawing rhythms from jazz and the blues, a poetry that with ironies and radical reversals generally avoids staginess; and poems of racial protest and definition. The jazz and blues poems have weathered rather less well than the protest poems. Written with white readers as well as black in mind, there is something missing from them – tonalities withheld, too much explication, a lack of candour about his sexuality and a guardedness in relation to his own as well as the white 'culture of reception'. The signals are there, the celebration of Whitman, 'Pleasured equally / In seeking as in finding'; the sailors, the ungendered poems and poems where deliberate stereotypes and personifications displace persons.

The vignettes use a Harlem idiom which brings character and circumstance alive. These are protest poems, but the more general, 'public' protest poems and some of the lyrics exploit a standard English when necessary, appropriate to the occasion; there is also power in using a language associated with repression to draw attention to the repressed. 'The Negro Speaks of Rivers' immediately inscribes itself in memory, its calm dignity and its universality giving it the clarity of voice and inscription at the same time. But the most famous and resonant of the protest poems is the affirmation 'I, too'. History has brought about its changes, but Hughes's poems of protest, still resonant, belong, unlike much protest poetry, to our moment as much as to their original time. More vehement, more radical poetry took up from where he left off, a poetry which became one with the events it catalyzed and interpreted. What makes Langston Hughes's poems durable is their confident-seeming delivery, a voice of affirmation rather than of struggle.

The Negro Speaks of Rivers

I've known rivers:
I've known rivers ancient as the world and older than the flow of human blood in
    human veins.
My soul has grown deep like the rivers.

I bathed in the Euphrates when dawns were young.
I built my hut near the Congo and it lulled me to sleep.
I looked upon the Nile and raised the pyramids above it.
I heard the singing of the Mississippi when Abe Lincoln went down to New Orleans,
    and I've seen its muddy bosom turn all golden in the sunset.

I've known rivers:
Ancient, dusky rivers.

My soul has grown deep like the rivers.

I built my hut near the Congo
and it lulled me to sleep.

My People

The night is beautiful,
So the faces of my people.

The stars are beautiful,
So the eyes of my people.

Beautiful, also, is the sun.
Beautiful, also, are the souls of my people.

Beautiful, also,
are the souls of my people.

Cross

My old man's a white old man
And my old mother's black.
If ever I cursed my white old man
I take my curses back.

If ever I cursed my black old mother
And wished she were in hell,
I'm sorry for that evil wish
And now I wish her well.

My old man died in a fine big house.
My ma died in a shack.
I wonder were I'm gonna die,
Being neither white nor black?

I too

I, too, sing America.

I am the darker brother.
They send me to eat in the kitchen
When company comes,
But I laugh,
And eat well,
And grow strong.

Tomorrow,
I'll be at the table
When company comes.
Nobody'll dare
Say to me,
'Eat in the kitchen,'
Then.

Besides,
They'll see how beautiful I am
And be ashamed—

I, too, am America.

I, too,
am America.

John
Betjeman

(1906–1984)

John Betjeman, an only child, was born John Betjemann in 1906 in London. His father was a cabinet maker of German extraction. During the First World War the Betjemans shed their second 'n' in the interests of appearing less Teutonic. In his lonely, early years his closest friend was Archibald, a teddy bear, about which he later wrote *Archie and the Strict Baptists*. He was sent to boarding school at the age of 11. Family holidays spent at Trebetherick, Cornwall, were happy times. Some of his poems are set in that landscape, and he kept returning for the rest of his days. He died there in 1984 and was buried at St.Enodoc's.

He went to Magdalen College, Oxford, in 1925 where the delights of undergraduate life precluded his completing a degree. W.H. Auden, his contemporary, was setting off for the 'World' while Betjeman was setting off for 'Britain', and more narrowly, 'England'. He was to develop in Britain a larger popular readership than Auden's: his 1958 *Collected Poems* was a run-away best-seller. But his work does not export as well as Auden's does.

After Oxford he became a schoolteacher, a secretary, an editor, a film critic, a writer. In 1931 his first book of poems appeared and soon after he married Penelope, daughter of Field Marshal Lord Chetwode, a formidable figure, previously Commander-in-Chief in India, who did not warm to his son-in-law. Yet the poet's writing, on landscape, architecture and the like was to have a decisive, conservative impact, and his broadcasts describing imperilled architectural treasures raised public awareness of history and heritage. Betjeman was a writer for the non-specialist, whether in verse or prose.

Though he uses conventional forms, his verse has a distinctive mark. This is due to more than recurrent subjects: churches, suburbia and gym-slips. There is throughout a kind of propriety. The satires bear his hallmark too: irony of tone and of detail. Rhythm is *lightly* controlled. Almost everywhere there is humour, tactful even when it is dark. Light verse of this order is rare; and light verse need not be unserious.

For example, 'I SIT DOWN/In St Botolph Bishopsgate Churchyard/And wait for the spirit of my grandfather/Toddling along from the Barbican.' Simple though this may be – it is impossible not to read on. He creates suspense in narrative and rhythm, a curiosity we follow up. He can be bleak: lonely, terrified of death, he takes Anglican consolation as it comes. He abhors the destruction of beautiful things, old habits of courtesy, old buildings, the Downs, poetic discipline. Satire is as much his duty as elegy and celebration.

A sense of place (what he calls 'a topographical predilection') is conveyed in each poem. In the love poems he sends up the speaker whose feelings of physical inferiority translate his substantial women into Amazons. 'Little, alas, to you I mean,/For I am bald, and old, and green.' He wants to be crushed in smooth strong arms or pressed to a glowing bosom. 'Pam, I adore you, you great big mountainous sportsgirl,' he declares. In 'The Licorice Fields of Pontefract' he writes: 'Her sturdy legs were flannel-slack'd,/The strongest legs in Pontefract.' The poet is 'held in brown arms strong and bare/And wound with flaming ropes of hair'. With economy he evokes these girls, evokes whole scenes and the society and value systems that underpin them.

His verse autobiography, *Summoned by Bells*, was, like his *Collected Poems*, a best seller. His broadcasting career during the 1960s and 1970s included memorable documentaries, *Metroland* and *A Passion for Churches*. In 1969 he was knighted and in 1973 he became Poet Laureate.

The Plantster's Vision

Cut down that timber! Bells, too many and strong,
　Pouring their music through the branches bare,
　From moon-white church towers down the windy air
Have pealed the centuries out with Evensong.
Remove those cottages, a huddled throng!
　Too many babies have been born in there,
　Too many coffins, bumping down the stair,
Carried the old their garden paths along.

I have a Vision of The Future, chum,
　The workers' flats in fields of soya beans
　　Tower up like silver pencils, score on score:
And Surging Millions hear the Challenge come
　From microphones in communal canteens
　　'No Right! No Wrong! All's perfect, evermore!'

The Licorice Fields at Pontefract

In the licorice fields at Pontefract
　My love and I did meet
And many a burdened licorice bush
　Was blooming round our feet;
Red hair she had and golden skin,
Her sulky lips were shaped for sin,
Her sturdy legs were flannel-slack'd
The strongest legs in Pontefract.

The light and dangling licorice flowers
　Gave off the sweetest smells;
From various black Victorian towers
　The Sunday evening bells
Came pealing over dales and hills
And tanneries and silent mills
And lowly streets where country stops
And little shuttered corner shops.

She cast her blazing eyes on me
　And plucked a licorice leaf;
I was her captive slave and she
　My red-haired robber chief.
Oh love! for love I could not speak,
It left me winded, wilting, weak,
And held in brown arms strong and bare
And wound with flaming ropes of hair.

Her sulky lips
were shaped
for sin

The Last Laugh

I made hay while the sun shone.
　My work sold.
Now, if the harvest is over
　And the world cold,
Give me the bonus of laughter
　As I lose hold.

A Shropshire Lad

The gas was on in the Institute,
　The flare was up in the gym,
A man was running a mineral line,
　A lass was singing a hymn,
When Captain Webb the Dawley man,
　Captain Webb from Dawley,
Came swimming along the old canal
　That carried the bricks to Lawley.
　　Swimming along —
　　Swimming along —
　　Swimming along from Severn,
And paying a call at Dawley Bank while swimming along to Heaven.

The sun shone low on the railway line
　And over the bricks and stacks
And in at the upstairs windows
　Of the Dawley houses' backs
When we saw the ghost of Captain Webb,
　Webb in a water sheeting,
Come dripping along in a bathing dress
　To the Saturday evening meeting.
　　Dripping along —
　　Dripping along —
　　To the Congregational Hall;
Dripping and still he rose over the sill and faded away in a wall.

There wasn't a man in Oakengates
　That hadn't got hold of the tale,
And over the valley in Ironbridge,
　And round by Coalbrookdale,
How Captain Webb the Dawley man,
　Captain Webb from Dawley,
Rose rigid and dead from the old canal
　That carries the bricks to Lawley.
　　Rigid and dead —
　　Rigid and dead —
　　To the Saturday congregation,
Paying a call at Dawley Bank on the way to his destination.

Dripping and still he rose over the sill and faded away in a wall.

W.H. Auden

(1907–1973)

Stop all the Clocks

Lullaby

Musée des Beaux Arts

The Shield of Achilles

In 1937 W.H. Auden was 30. He was the leading poet of his generation; his name had spread to America. He was the voice of youth, the voice of the radical left, well-travelled and widely respected. A double issue of the magazine *New Verse* was dedicated to him. Dylan Thomas contributed ambiguous words. 'I think of Mr Auden's poetry as a hygiene, a knowledge and practice, based on a brilliantly prejudiced analysis of contemporary disorders, relating to the preservation and promotion of health, a sanitary science and a flusher of melancholia.'

The prejudice was political: a Communist who wrote reviews and articles for the Communist press; a sentimentalist when it came to the industrial landscape and industry; a man of prejudice, the kind that attaches to privileges of education and class, expressing itself in a distinct tone of voice and in the patterning of the verse. The contemporary disorders are political: the failure to square up to Fascism and Nazism, the failure to alter the social structure after the reversals of the Depression, the failure to end Empire; and, within the moral structure of his own 1930s generation, a disorder, an intolerance of things dear to him, not least his sexual nature.

Wystan Hugh Auden was born in York. His father was a doctor and for Auden 'medicine', the human body and the body politic, were a rich source of imagery. His mother, a musical woman, encouraged her son. While his father was away at war, she and young Wystan sang together at the piano – Wagner, *Tristan und Isolde*, with the boy taking Isolde's part. In later life Auden wrote for music, notably the incomparable libretto for Igor Stravinsky's *The Rake's Progress.*

He spent the years from six to 12 creating 'a private secondary world' of limestone landscapes, lead mines and workings. He learned from his secondary worlds 'certain principles' that applied 'to all artistic fabrication'. Every work of art was a secondary world derived from and answerable to the primary world. Consistent, even if arbitrary rules were necessary in the 'game' of making. Within those rules the poet 'must never make a statement simply because it sounds poetically exciting; he must also believe it to be true'.

He was sent to preparatory school in Norfolk, and then to public school where he studied biology. At 15 he discovered by accident his poetic vocation and in 1925 went up to Christ Church, Oxford to read English. He was drawn to Old English poetry and his early technical experiments in stress and alliterative forms developed from there. Soon his books began to appear, starting in 1930 with *Poems* and *Paid on Both Sides: A Charade.*

In 1939 he emigrated to the United States – it was time, he decided, to find himself. *Another Time* (1940) contained the last of Auden's English poems. In 1946 he became an American citizen. He certainly changed. But, early and late, what marks Auden is a refusal to conform, to come down from his linguistic and cultural perch, to 'trim'. 'What is a highbrow?' he asks in an early piece. 'Someone who is not passive to his experience but who tries to organize, explain and alter it, someone in fact, who tries to influence his history...'

He affected his successors, marking out the ironic spaces in which many compose their poems. Hardy, his great early example, spoke of life's ironies, the way fate confronted man. For Auden irony is not a thematic verity but a stylistic device, an instrument of obliquity with which to explore difficult subjects without getting too close.

Stop all the Clocks

Stop all the clocks, cut off the telephone,
Prevent the dog from barking with a juicy bone,
Silence the pianos and with muffled drum
Bring out the coffin, let the mourners come.

Let aeroplanes circle moaning overhead
Scribbling on the sky the message He Is Dead,
Put crêpe bows round the white necks of the public doves,
Let the traffic policemen wear black cotton gloves.

He was my North, my South, my East and West,
My working week and my Sunday rest,
My noon, my midnight, my talk, my song;
I thought that love would last for ever: I was wrong.

The stars are not wanted now: put out every one;
Pack up the moon and dismantle the sun;
Pour away the ocean and sweep up the wood.
For nothing now can ever come to any good.

> I thought
> that love
> would last
> for ever:
> I was wrong.

Lullaby

Lay your sleeping head, my love,
Human on my faithless arm;
Time and fevers burn away
Individual beauty from
Thoughtful children, and the grave
Proves the child ephemeral:
But in my arms till break of day
Let the living creature lie,
Mortal, guilty, but to me
The entirely beautiful.

Soul and body have no bounds:
To lovers as they lie upon
Her tolerant enchanted slope
In their ordinary swoon,
Grave the vision Venus sends
Of supernatural sympathy,
Universal love and hope;
While abstract insight wakes
Among the glaciers and the rocks
The hermit's sensual ecstasy.

Certainty, fidelity
On the stroke of midnight pass
Like vibrations of a bell,
And fashionable madmen raise
Their pedantic boring cry:
Every farthing of the cost,
All the dreaded cards foretell,
Shall be paid, but from this night
Not a whisper, not a thought,
Not a kiss nor look be lost.

Beauty, midnight, vision dies:
Let the winds of dawn that blow
Softly round your dreaming head
Such a day of sweetness show
Eye and knocking heart may bless,
Find your mortal world enough;
Noons of dryness see you fed
By the involuntary powers,
Nights of insult let you pass
Watched by every human love.

Musée des Beaux Arts

About suffering they were never wrong,

The Old Masters; how well they understood

Its human position; how it takes place

While someone else is eating or opening a window or just walking dully along;

How, when the aged are reverently, passionately waiting

For the miraculous birth, there always must be

Children who did not specially want it to happen, skating

On a pond at the edge of the wood:

They never forgot

That even the dreadful martyrdom must run its course

Anyhow in a corner, some untidy spot

Where the dogs go on with their doggy life and the torturer's horse

Scratches its innocent behind on a tree.

In Breughel's *Icarus*, for instance: how everything turns away

Quite leisurely from the disaster; the ploughman may

Have heard the splash, the forsaken cry,

But for him it was not an important failure; the sun shone

As it had to on the white legs disappearing into the green

Water; and the expensive delicate ship that must have seen

Something amazing, a boy falling out of the sky,

had somewhere to get to and sailed calmly on.

Anyhow in a corner, some untidy spot
Where the dogs go on with their doggy
life and the torturer's horse
Scratches its innocent behind on a tree.

The Shield of Achilles

She looked over his shoulder
　　For vines and olive trees,
Marble well-governed cities
　　And ships upon untamed seas,
But there on the shining metal
　　His hands had put instead
An artificial wilderness
　　And a sky like lead.

A plain without a feature, bare and brown,
　　No blade of grass, no sign of neighbourhood,
Nothing to eat and nowhere to sit down,
　　Yet, congregated on its blankness, stood
　　An unintelligible multitude,
A million eyes, a million boots in line,
Without expression, waiting for a sign.

Out of the air a voice without a face
　　Proved by statistics that some cause was just
In tones as dry and level as the place:
　　No one was cheered and nothing was discussed;
　　Column by column in a cloud of dust
They marched away enduring a belief
Whose logic brought them, somewhere else, to grief.

She looked over his shoulder
　　For ritual pieties,
White flower-garlanded heifers,
　　Libation and sacrifice,
But there on the shining metal
　　Where the altar should have been,
She saw by his flickering forge-light
　　Quite another scene.

Barbed wire enclosed an arbitrary spot
　　Where bored officials lounged (one cracked a joke)
And sentries sweated for the day was hot:
　　A crowd of ordinary decent folk
　　Watched from without and neither moved nor spoke
As three pale figures were led forth and bound
To three posts driven upright in the ground.

And sentries
sweated for the
day was hot

The mass and majesty of this world, all
    That carries weight and always weighs the same
Lay in the hands of others; they were small
    And could not hope for help and no help came:
    What their foes like to do was done, their shame
Was all the worst could wish; they lost their pride
And died as men before their bodies died.

      She looked over his shoulder
        For athletes at their games,
      Men and women in a dance
        Moving their sweet limbs
      Quick, quick, to music.
        But there on the shining shield
      His hands had set no dancing-floor
        But a weed-choked field.

A ragged urchin, aimless and alone,
    Loitered about that vacancy; a bird
Flew up to safety from his well-aimed stone:
    That girls are raped, that two boys knife a third,
    Were axioms to him, who'd never heard
Of any world where promises were kept,
Or one could weep because another wept.

      The thin-lipped armorer,
        Hephaestos, hobbled away,
      Thetis of the shining breasts
        Cried out in dismay
      At what the god had wrought
        To please her son, the strong
      Iron-hearted man-slaying Achilles
        Who would not live long.

And died as men before their bodies died.

Elizabeth
Bishop
(1911–1979)

Over 2,000 Illustrations and a
Complete Concordance

In 1946, reviewing *North & South*, Marianne Moore declared: 'Elizabeth Bishop is spectacular in being unspectacular.' Bishop took her early bearings from Moore, an invaluable apprenticeship, and she kept faith with Moore as long as she could, until she recognized how different their reticences were. And Moore continued to admire qualities in Bishop: 'Some authors do not muse within themselves; they "think" – like the vegetable-shredder which cuts into the life of a thing. Miss Bishop is not one of these frettingly intensive machines. Yet the rational considering quality in her work is its strength – assisted by unwordiness, uncontorted intenionalness, the flicker of impudence, the natural unforced ending.'

Born in Worcester, Massachusetts, Elizabeth Bishop's early years were hard. Her father died when she was eight months old, her mother was committed to a mental institution when she was five. She was reared by her mother's parents in Nova Scotia and by an aunt in Boston. She graduated from Vassar College in 1934. Her life was given over to travel: to Florida, Europe, Mexico and Brazil, where she lived for many years. For her, travel is an activity in which to get lost (and found): time's tyranny is loosened; in travel connections occur, and connection is epiphany, an area of understanding. Her final years were spent in Cambridge, Massachusetts, where she taught and where she died.

After Moore, her closest poetic connection was with Robert Lowell. They maintained a candid and affectionate exchange, willing to offer severe criticism when they felt it was required. He celebrated her with fascinated affection in *Notebook* (1970), where he considered her meticulous, patient method of composition

> Have you ever seen an inchworm crawl up a leaf,
> cling to the very end, revolve in air,
> feeling for something to reach something? My dear,
> you hang your words in air, years old, imperfect,
> pasted to cardboard posters, gay lettered, gapped
> for the unimagined phrases and the wide-eyed Muse,
> uneasy caller, finds her casual friend.

The longing to find rather than forge connections between experiences, with a beloved, a landscape or the past, provides the dynamic of her poems. She looks and looks with such attention that what she sees is almost surrealized: 'glimpses of the always more successful surrealism of everyday life', Randall Jarrell says, 'all her poems have written underneath, *I have seen it*', and seen it with wry and anxious interrogation. The voice affirms, hesitates, corrects itself; the image comes clear to us as it came clear to her, a process of adjusting perception until the thing is in focus, but enriched by the process of focusing.

The enabling instrument in Bishop's poems is the syntax, not always dancing on its points, like Moore's, but seemingly casual, barefoot. The effect is intimate, rapt, the voice always subject-defined, its repetitions and qualifications building towards a precise sense of that subject. Few poets are as candid as Elizabeth Bishop. We learn more of her from her poems, despite her reticence, her refusal to confess or provide personal detail, than we do of Plath, Lowell or Sexton from theirs. They dramatize and partialize themselves. Bishop asks us to focus not *on* but *with* her. Her disclosures are tactful: we can recognize them if we wish. Her reticence is 'polite'. Given her vulnerability, she could have 'gone to the edge'. Instead, her poetry finds a way back.

Thus should have been our travels:
serious, engravable.
The Seven Wonders of the World are tired
and a touch familiar, but the other scenes,
innumerable, though equally sad and still,
are foreign. Often the squatting Arab,
or group of Arabs, plotting, probably,
against our Christian Empire,
while one apart, with outstretched arm and hand
points to the Tomb, the Pit, the Sepulcher.
The branches of the date-palms look like files.
The cobbled courtyard, where the Well is dry,
is like a diagram, the brickwork conduits
are vast and obvious, the human figure
far gone in history or theology,
gone with its camel or its faithful horse.
Always the silence, the gesture, the specks of birds
suspended on invisible threads above the Site,
or the smoke rising solemnly, pulled by threads.
Granted a page alone or a page made up
of several scenes arranged in cattycornered rectangles
or circles set on stippled gray,
granted a grim lunette,
caught in the toils of an initial letter,
when dwelt upon, they all resolve themselves.
The eye drops, weighted, through the lines
the burin made, the lines that move apart
like ripples above sand,
dispersing storms, God's spreading fingerprint,
and painfully, finally, that ignite
in watery prismatic white-and-blue.

Entering the Narrows at St. Johns
the touching bleat of goats reached to the ship.
We glimpsed them, reddish, leaping up the cliffs
among the fog-soaked weeds and butter-and-eggs.
And at St. Peter's the wind blew and the sun shone madly.
Rapidly, purposefully, the Collegians marched in lines,
crisscrossing the great square with black, like ants.

Always the
silence,
the gesture,
the specks
of birds

In Mexico the dead man lay
in a blue arcade; the dead volcanoes
glistened like Easter lilies.
The jukebox went on playing 'Ay, Jalisco!'
And at Volubilis there were beautiful poppies
splitting the mosaics; the fat old guide made eyes.
In Dingle harbor a golden length of evening
the rotting hulks held up their dripping plush.
The Englishwoman poured tea, informing us
that the Duchess was going to have a baby.
And in the brothels of Marrakesh
the little pockmarked prostitutes
balanced their tea-trays on their heads
and did their belly-dances; flung themselves
naked and giggling against our knees,
asking for cigarettes. It was somewhere near there
I saw what frightened me most of all:
A holy grave, not looking particularly holy,
one of a group under a keyhole-arched stone baldaquin
open to every wind from the pink desert.
An open, gritty, marble trough, carved solid
with exhortation, yellowed
as scattered cattle-teeth;
half-filled with dust, not even the dust
of the poor prophet paynim who once lay there.
In a smart burnoose Khadour looked on amused.

Everything only connected by 'and' and 'and'.
Open the book. (The gilt rubs off the edges
of the pages and pollinates the fingertips.)
Open the heavy book. Why couldn't we have seen
this old Nativity while we were at it?
— the dark ajar, the rocks breaking with light,
an undisturbed, unbreathing flame,
colorless, sparkless, freely fed on straw,
and, lulled within, a family with pets,
— and looked and looked our infant sight away.

C.H. **Sisson**

(1914–2003)

C.H. Sisson was an outstanding (non-academic) critic, political theorist and a uniquely gifted translator and poet. With writers of his generation he shares what 'the movement' most distrusted – a faith in artistic instinct and a refusal to restrict the freedom of poetry by rule. He could write masterfully in traditional forms, but he reserved the liberty to write outside them as well. He remembers in adolescence how he would know a poem was about to happen to him, 'and I had not to think about it in case I should spoil it … there is probably something in the nature of poetry which makes it necessary to avoid conscious premeditation.'

In an essay on Charles Péguy he asks, 'Is not every sincere life, in a sense, a journey to the first years?' To Sisson the first years of a life, of a culture, beginnings, break-points and re-beginnings, matter. What does art transcend, how does it transcend? This is not to confuse biography with criticism. Criticism follows from it; biography clears a ground.

Charles Hubert Sisson was born in Bristol. His father was from Westmorland, his mother from Wiltshire. His father became a clock-maker and later, in Bristol, an optician. It was a meagre time. The landscapes that took hold of the poet were those of the West Country and of Somerset. He attended the University of Bristol, then studied in Germany and France when the forces of German militarism were gathering strength. He was anxious for France, and for England. He entered the Civil Service in 1936. The next year he married. He enlisted in 1942 and was sent for two and a half years to the North West Frontier Province. He translated Heine, read Dante and Virgil, and wrote the first of his mature poems.

In 1945 he resumed work in Whitehall, rising to Under Secretary and equivalent heights in the Ministry of Labour. He was rare among contemporary poets in his belief that a writer serves best as a man engaged with the social machine, guarding the integrity of social institutions on behalf of his fellow citizens, even as he criticizes and helps improve them. In 1972 he retired to Langport, Somerset, where he produced the bulk of his poetry and translations.

His poems can seem Augustan, reminiscent of the classical style of late seventeenth- and eighteenth-century English literature. However, his poetry does not follow the Augustan principle of trusting reason to explore experience: it establishes connections on the other side of reason, communicating to the pulse through distinctive rhythms. He quotes a French critic as saying 'reason may convince, but it is rhythm that persuades.' Rhythm is authority. In 'The Usk' this is amply demonstrated. Rhythm integrates diverse material – it performs feats of lucid fusion. Ezra Pound's example transformed Sisson's hearing, 'opening up a new area in consciousness', and caused 'one of those real adjustments of mind which even the most omnivorous reader can expect from only a few writers'.

In Sisson we encounter a wholly English writer, a man as English as MacDiarmid is Scottish or Heaney is Irish. That Englishness marks his work, from the satires to the autumnal and elegiac poems with which his life's work ended. The 'technique of ignorance' which a poet must cultivate if he wishes to tell the truth leads, for a moment, to a stream of commonalty that flows variously, that 'for a moment' manages to say 'that which is'.

The Usk

Christ is the language which we speak to God
And also God, so that we speak in truth;
He in us, we in him, speaking
To one another, to him, the City of God.

I

Such a fool as I am you had better ignore
Tongue twist, malevolent, fat mouthed
I have no language but that other one
His the Devil's, no mouse I, creeping out of the cheese
With a peaked cap scanning the distance
Looking for truth.
Words when I have them, come out, the Devil
Encouraging, grinning from the other side of the street
And my tears
Streaming, a blubbered face, when I am not laughing
Where in all this
Is calm, measure,
Exactness
The Lord's peace?

II

Nothing is in my own voice because I have not
Any. Nothing in my own name
Here inscribed on water, nothing but flow
A ripple, outwards. Standing beside the Usk
You flow like truth, river, I will get in
Over me, through me perhaps, river let me be crystalline
As I shall not be, shivering upon the bank.
A swan passed. So is it, the surface, sometimes
Benign like a mirror, but not I passing, the bird.

III

Under the bridge, meet reward, the water
Falling in cascades or worse, you devil, for truthfulness
Is no part of the illusion, the clear sky
Is not yours, the water
Falling not yours
Only the sheep
Munching at the river brim
Perhaps

IV

What I had hoped for, the clear line
Tremulous like water but
Clear also to the stones underneath
Has not come that way, for my truth
Was not public enough, nor perhaps true.

A ripple,
outwards.
Standing
beside the Usk

Holy Father, Almighty God
Stop me before I speak

          —per Christum.

     V

Lies on my tongue. Get up and bolt the door
For I am coming not to be believed
The messenger of anything I say.
So I am come, stand in the cold tonight
The servant of the grain upon my tongue,
Beware, I am the man, and let me in.

      VI

So speech is treasured, for the things it gives
Which I can not have, for I speak too plain
Yet not so plain as to be understood
It is confusion and a madman's tongue.
Where drops the reason, there is no one by.
Torture my mind: and so swim through the night
As envy cannot touch you, or myself
Sleep comes, and let her, warm at my side, like death.
The Holy Spirit and the Holy One
Of Israel be my guide. So among tombs
Truth may be sought, and found, if we rejoice
With Ham and Shem and Japhet in the dark
The ark rolls onward over a wide sea.
Come sleep, come lightning, comes the dove at last.

Beware,
I am the
man, and
let me in.

Anchises

This is my proper sightlessness,
The invisible pack hunting the visible air.
There are those who exist, but it is not I.
Existent are: bodies, although their existence is
Not proven; tremors
Through the vast air expecting some other thing
Not known, or hopeless; or else hoped for and lost.
One could devise invisibility,
Walking by it as if it were not obligatory
As it is with me, *moi qui n'existe pas*
Non sum, therefore *non cogito*, though there are shapes
Upon a mind I sometimes take to be mine.
This is not much to show for sixty years
Here by the Latin gate, or where the Baltic
Spreads its white arms over the barren sand.
Do not number me on this seashore
Where the effete light from the north
Floods over the ice-cap. I came from Troy
It was not after she had ended, but before.

Dylan
Thomas
(1914–1953)

The Hand that Signed …
The Force that Through …
A Refusal to Mourn …
Do Not Go Gentle …

Dylan Marlais Thomas wrote always just beyond his considerable, instinctive understanding. He dazzled himself and, in performance, conveyed the dazzle to his audience. He was born in Swansea, Wales. His father was a schoolmaster and poet who recited Shakespeare to the boy before he could read. His placid mother was devoted to him. He remembers an early infatuation with the sound of nursery rhymes – the 'colours' words suggested to him and the exciting rhythms. This apprenticeship to Mother Goose predisposed him to highly rhythmic poetry.

He attended the grammar school where his father was senior English master. A short boy, he was competitive and wanted to be best or worst at everything. At 17 he left school and became a newspaper reporter. After 15 months he returned home and between 1932 and 1934 composed well over half the poems he published during his lifetime. He enjoyed dissolute roles in amateur theatricals: role playing became a habit, only – as Robert Nye says – 'none of the masks quite fit.'

Eighteen Poems appeared in 1934, followed two years later by *Twenty-Five Poems*, and in 1939 *The Map of Love* with prose and verse rounded off his early career. The collections are much of a piece and many regard them as the best of Thomas; they are more individually his than the prophetic, less obscure work of his most famous book, *Deaths and Entrances* (1946). During the war he did work for the BBC, publishing an autobiography, *Portrait of the Artist as a Young Dog*, in 1940. He died in 1953, aged 39, during an American lecture tour.

Describing his technique to a young fan, he wrote: 'I make an image – though "make" is not the right word; I let, perhaps, an image be "made" emotionally in me and then apply to it what intellectual and critical forces I possess – let it breed another, let that image contradict the first, make, of the third image bred out of the other two together, a fourth contradictory image, and let them all, within my imposed formal limits, conflict.' From conflicting images, as much the product of will as of imagination, he tries to generate 'that momentary peace which is a poem'.

'He is shut in the twisted tower of his own observation,' says Nye, 'a tower where only words are real and can bleed' – seldom words that signify specific meanings, but words as peep-holes through to a world of analogies. He is addicted to synaesthesia – he sees sounds and hears sights. Words suggest, they don't denote. It is a thoroughgoing and seductive aesthetic, and the elegiac eroticism of Thomas's early poems is heady, adolescent stuff. The poems often appear to be 'about' masturbation, the occasion behind a hedge of repeated syntactical constructions, rhythmic repetitions and the intensive vocabulary unsustained by intense rhythm. 'And time set forth my mortal creature / To drift and drown upon the sea' means 'I was born' – after five stanzas of lurid gestation – and 'I shall die' after one more stanza.

His poems, closely observed, can seem like a fullness masking an emptiness. Not that we doubt the sincerity of his feelings: we doubt the sincerity and the probity of the poem, as we doubt poems which borrow their rhetoric from, for example, the holocaust. Thomas weaves spells. He engages language, rather than experience. When the spell releases us, nothing is clarified, but something magical has happened. His poetry responds to analysis the way a puzzle might, but beyond the puzzlement is the magic.

The Hand that Signed …

The hand that signed the paper felled a city;
Five sovereign fingers taxed the breath,
Doubled the globe of dead and halved a country;
These five kings did a king to death.

The mighty hand leads to a sloping shoulder,
The finger joints are cramped with chalk;
A goose's quill has put an end to murder
That put an end to talk.

The hand that signed the treaty bred a fever,
And famine grew, and locusts came;
Great is the hand that holds dominion over
Man by a scribbled name.

The five kings count the dead but do not soften
The crusted wound nor stroke the brow;
A hand rules pity as a hand rules heaven;
Hands have no tears to flow.

These five
kings did a
king to death.

The Force that Through …

The force that through the green fuse drives the flower
Drives my green age; that blasts the roots of trees
    Is my destroyer.
And I am dumb to tell the crooked rose
My youth is bent by the same wintry fever.

The force that drives the water through the rocks
Drives my red blood; that dries the mouthing streams
    Turns mine to wax.
And I am dumb to mouth unto my veins
How at the mountain spring the same mouth sucks.

The hand that whirls the water in the pool
Stirs the quicksand; that ropes the blowing wind
    Hauls my shroud sail.
And I am dumb to tell the hanging man
How of my clay is made the hangman's lime.

The lips of time leech to the fountain head;
Love drips and gathers, but the fallen blood
    Shall calm her sores.
And I am dumb to tell a weather's wind
How time has ticked a heaven round the stars.

And I am dumb to tell the lover's tomb
How at my sheet goes the same crooked worm.

A Refusal to Mourn …

Never until the mankind making
    Bird beast and flower
Fathering and all humbling darkness
Tells with silence the last light breaking
    And the still hour
Is come of the sea tumbling in harness

And I must enter again the round
    Zion of the water bead
And the synagogue of the ear of corn
Shall I let pray the shadow of a sound
    Or sow my salt seed
In the least valley of sackcloth to mourn

The majesty and burning of the child's death.
    I shall not murder
The mankind of her going with a grave truth
Nor blaspheme down the stations of the breath
    With any further
Elegy of innocence and youth.

Deep with the first dead lies London's daughter,
    Robed in the long friends,
The grains beyond age, the dark veins of her mother,
Secret by the unmourning water
    Of the riding Thames.
After the first death, there is no other.

The grains
beyond age,
the dark
veins of her
mother

Do Not Go Gentle …

Do not go gentle into that good night,
Old age should burn and rave at close of day;
Rage, rage against the dying of the light.

Though wise men at their end know dark is right,
Because their words had forked no lightning they
Do not go gentle into that good night.

Good men, the last wave by, crying how bright
Their frail deeds might have danced in a green bay,
Rage, rage against the dying of the light.

Wild men who caught and sang the sun in flight,
And learn, too late, they grieved it on its way,
Do not go gentle into that good night.

Grave men, near death, who see with blinding sight
Blind eyes could blaze like meteors and be gay,
Rage, rage against the dying of the light.

And you, my father, there on that sad height,
Curse, bless, me now with your fierce tears, I pray.
Do not go gentle into that good night.
Rage, rage against the dying of the light.

Robert
Lowell
(1917–1977)

Home after Three Months Away

For the Union Dead

Epilogue

In an age of prurience, poets who deal the pay-dirt on themselves, referred to since Robert Lowell's *Life Studies* (1959) as 'confessional poets', are an inevitable phenomenon. Poets have always complained, settled scores and licked their wounds, but not for the most part opened their wounds and probed them before readers. What does 'confessional poetry' entail? Why must confession always suggest negative testimony? A poet might as well confess good as bad qualities. The virtue of Lowell's poetry is in its apparent candour.

'Confessional' suggests religion as well: a poet on his way to penance and sacramental absolution, the possible reparation and forgiveness. Lowell understood the sacramental side from his Roman Catholic years when he spent days at a time in prayer. The heart must be contrite, the posture humble. It doesn't call good deeds and impulses into the account, though they should be part of any sacrament of self-recognition. Confession is not an end: it leads to communion and back to community.

In confessional poetry this is not the pattern. Lowell is unusual in the mercilessness of his verse, but also in the way he makes his situation generally pertinent, even characteristic, of his age, class and gender. Details come together – a trail of cruel sparks illuminates past and future, yet cannot be controlled. When religious belief is in abeyance, who can we turn to, in what terms can we speak? In literal details, or – the alternative strategy which Sylvia Plath devised – in symbolic narratives.

Lowell was born in Boston into an undistinguished branch of a distinguished 'aristocratic' Boston family with substantial political and cultural connections. He had a strong mother and a cardboard father. At his exclusive school he was nicknamed Caligula because of his unpredictability and cruelty; the nickname 'Cal' stayed with him for life. He went to Harvard and then, rebelling against his family and his privileged culture, transferred to Kenyon College to study with John Crowe Ransom and Allen Tate. In 1940 he graduated in Classics and, furthering his rebellion, became a Roman Catholic. Three years later, in protest against the allied bombing of European cities, he became a conscientious objector and spent time in detention, again to the horror of his family. His first book appeared in 1944; his second, *Lord Weary's Castle*, appeared in 1946 when he was 29 and won a Pulitzer Prize. He was clearly the major figure in American poetry.

Life Studies marked a definitive break for him and for American and – subsequently – the other English poetries. A suffering mad self is his subject, with its antecedent selves and the uncomprehended other selves around it – lovers, wife, family, friends, fellow inmates in asylums, figures from history – all fodder for *Life Studies* – the title insists on the actuality of the circumstances and characters. They are transformed into rather than out of themselves.

His 1964 volume, *For the Union Dead*, united critics around him. Here the vulnerability of relationships and values is eloquently and politically explored. His confession is circumstantial, full of the contingent world – not solipsism or exorcism but a going into. He restlessly revised his earlier work; there was fluidity in his texts as he redeveloped them again and again. Memory and imagination became snagged together, both tragically and fruitfully. That was the big paradox of the life that produced the hundreds of small paradoxes in the later poems: 'All's misalliance.' Fretful, torn between Europe and America, in 1977 he died in a taxi from Kennedy Airport in New York. Having seen all the symptoms in his society and in himself, he succumbed to them.

Home after Three Months Away

Gone now the baby's nurse,
a lioness who ruled the roost
and made the Mother cry.
She used to tie
gobbets of porkrind in bowknots of gauze—
three months they hung like soggy toast
on our eight foot magnolia tree,
and helped the English sparrows
weather a Boston winter.

Three months, three months!
Is Richard now himself again?
Dimpled with exaltation,
my daughter holds her levee in the tub.
Our noses rub,
each of us pats a stringy lock of hair—
they tell me nothing's gone.
Though I am forty-one,
not forty now, the time I put away
was child's-play. After thirteen weeks
my child still dabs her cheeks
to start me shaving. When
we dress her in her sky-blue corduroy,
she changes to a boy,
and floats my shaving brush
and washcloth in the flush…
Dearest, I cannot loiter here
in lather like a polar bear.

Recuperating, I neither spin nor toil.
Three storeys down below,
a choreman tends our coffin's length of soil,
and seven horizontal tulips blow.
Just twelve months ago,
these flowers were pedigreed
imported Dutchmen; now no one need
distinguish them from weed.
Bushed by the late spring snow,
they cannot meet
another year's snowballing enervation.

I keep no rank nor station.
Cured, I am frizzled, stale and small.

Dearest,
I cannot
loiter here
in lather like
a polar bear.

For the Union Dead

Relinquunt Ommia Servare Rem Publicam.

The old South Boston Aquarium stands
in a Sahara of snow now. Its broken windows are boarded:
The bronze weathervane cod has lost half its scales.
The airy tanks are dry.

Once my nose crawled like a snail on the glass;
my hand tingled
to burst the bubbles
drifting from the noses of the cowed, compliant fish.

My hand draws back. I often sigh still
for the dark downward and vegetating kingdom
of the fish and reptile. One morning last March,
I pressed against the new barbed and galvanized

fence on the Boston Common. Behind their cage,
yellow dinosaur steamshovels were grunting
as they cropped up tons of mush and grass
to gouge their underworld garage.

Parking spaces luxuriate like civic
sandpiles in the heart of Boston.
A girdle of orange, Puritan-pumpkin colored girders
braces the tingling Statehouse,

shaking over the excavations, as it faces Colonel Shaw
and his bell-cheeked Negro infantry
on St. Gaudens shaking Civil War relief,
propped by a plank splint against the garage's earthquake.

Two months after marching through Boston,
half the regiment was dead;
at the dedication,
William James could almost hear the bronze Negroes breathe.

Their monument sticks like a fishbone
in the city's throat.
Its Colonel is as lean
as a compass-needle.

He has an angry wrenlike vigilance,
a greyhound's gentle tautness;
he seems to wince at pleasure,
and suffocate for privacy.

The bronze weather-vane cod has lost half its scales.

He is out of bounds now. He rejoices in man's lovely,
peculiar power to choose life and die—
when he leads his black soldiers to death,
he cannot bend his back.

On a thousand small town New England greens,
the old white churches hold their air
of sparse, sincere rebellion; frayed flags
quilt the graveyards of the Grand Army of the Republic.

The stone statutes of the abstract Union Soldier
grow slimmer and younger each year—
wasp-waisted, they doze over muskets
and muse through their sideburns…

Shaw's father wanted no monument
except the ditch,
where his son's body was thrown
and lost with his 'niggers.'

The ditch is nearer.
There are no statues for the last war here;
on Boylston Street, a commercial photograph
shows Hiroshima boiling

over a Mosler Safe, the 'Rock of Ages'
that survived the blast. Space is nearer.
When I crouch to my television set,
the drained faces of Negro school-children rise like balloons.

Colonel Shaw
is riding on his bubble,
he waits
for the blesséd break.

The Aquarium is gone. Everywhere,
giant finned cars nose forward like fish;
a savage servility
slides by on grease.

the drained faces of Negro school-
children rise like balloons.

Epilogue

Those blessèd structures, plot and rhyme—
why are they no help to me now
I want to make
something imagined, not recalled?
I hear the noise of my own voice.
The painter's vision is not a lens:
it trembles to caress the light.
But sometimes everything I write
with the threadbare art of my eye
seems a snapshot,
lurid, rapid, garish, grouped,
heightened from life,
yet paralyzed by fact.
All's misalliance.
Yet why not say what happened?
Pray for the grace of accuracy
Vermeer gave to the sun's illumination
stealing like the tide across a map
to his girl solid with yearning.
We are poor passing facts,
warned by that to give
each figure in the photograph
his living name.

We are poor passing facts,
warned by that to give
each figure in the photograph
his living name.

W.S.
Graham
(1918–1986)

Gigha

Imagine a Forest

I leave this at your ear for when you wake …

William Sydney Graham was born in a tenement in Greenock, Scotland, 'beside the sugar house quays', as he says – a run-down urban setting, open to the sea. He was of 'unlettered' origins. The sea dominates the imagery of his poems, whether calm, in flood or frozen. He remained a Celt, moving from Scotland, via London, to Cornwall where he found seascapes without urban clutter, just the occasional ruined tin-mine with its sad rhetoric. There is a 'Scots timbre' to Graham's voice, and he shares with Hugh MacDiarmid, his master for a time, a suppleness in tonal change, from raucous to tender, from elegy to anger and back again.

He attended Greenock High School, later spending a year at the Workers' Educational Association College near Edinburgh. He acquired no further formal education though he briefly became an academic in 1947–8, teaching at New York University. By that time he had published three collections, starting with *Cage Without Grievance* in 1942.

All of his poems have a location, a plot and setting (or a narrative). We have to infer the location and narrative poem by poem. It was with *The Nightfishing* (1955) that he finally found his poetic stride. But he vanished from sight and was presumed dead until he reappeared in the late 1960s and *Malcolm Mooney's Land* was published in 1970, a triumphant return to visibility. He has been on the map ever since.

The first act of engagement of reader and poem, Graham insisted, was in reading it aloud. This tested the syntax, pace and tone of poem and reader. Many of the poems are about making the noise of poems, how words enter another mouth and are shaped and emitted by other lips, how they change, and change the reader.

Graham was always troubled by the discontinuity of the 'I' – the self who writes the poem – who, year by year, day by day, looks back at earlier poems unable to make contact with them. In the end it is less the fluid identity that obsesses him: it is Time. What we write today stays written from where we wrote it, so that tomorrow or ten years later we come upon it and it speaks from where we were with all that we were then and are no more. He resents the 'timeless' stability of the art object while the artist remains time-bound.

His other themes include, in his words, 'the lessons in physical phenomena; the mystery and adequacy of the aesthetic experience; the elation of being alive in the language'. He experiments with sudden simple, largely monosyllabic lines. He begins using erratic but effective rhyme and slant rhyme. The movement is towards the three-stress ballad line.

Graham lived through three phases. In the first he had no sense of audience, being word-drunk, not sentence or cadence drunk. There were no voices – just crammed word-packages. In the second phase, he developed the sense of a single listener or a small audience, discovering the supple value of syntax combined with simple diction. A voice spoke, eccentric, beguiling, which we are content to follow into areas of obscurity and incomprehension; content, because the rhythms compel us to continue reading the poems despite any difficulties in understanding them. In the late poems (the third phase), aware of readership at last, he begins to prattle, becoming at times a mere self-intoxicated voice, at times more compelling than ever before.

Gigha

That firewood pale with salt and burning green
Outfloats its men who waved with a sound of drowning
Their saltcut hands over mazes of this rough bay.

Quietly this morning beside the subsided herds
Of water I walk. The children wade the shallows.
The sun with long legs wades into the sea.

Imagine a Forest

Imagine a forest
A real forest.

You are walking in it and it sighs
Round you where you go in a deep
Ballad on the border of a time
You have seemed to walk in before.
It is nightfall and you go through
Trying to find between the twittering
Shades the early starlight edge
Of the open moor land you know.
I have set you here and it is not a dream
I put you through. Go on between
The elephant bark of those beeches
Into that lightening, almost glade.

And he has taken
My word and gone

Through his own Ettrick darkening
Upon himself and he's come across
A glinted knight lying dying
On needles under a high tree.
Ease his visor open gently
To reveal whatever white, encased
Face will ask out at you who
It is you are or if you will
Finish him off. His eyes are open.
Imagine he does not speak. Only
His beard moving against the metal
Signs that he would like to speak.

> A glinted
> knight lying
> dying
> On needles
> under a
> high tree.

Imagine a room
Where you are home

Taking your boots off from the wood
In that deep ballad very not
A dream and the fire noisily
Kindling up and breaking its sticks.
Do not imagine I put you there
For nothing. I put you through it
There in that holt of words between
The bearded liveoaks and the beeches
For you to meet a man alone
Slipping out of whatever cause
He thought he lay there dying for.

Hang up the ballad
Behind the door.

You are come home but you are about
To not fight hard enough and die
In a no less desolate dark wood
Where a stranger shall never enter.

Imagine a forest
A real forest.

The bearded liveoaks and the beeches

I leave this at your ear for when you wake …

I leave this at your ear for when you wake,
A creature in its abstract cage asleep.
Your dreams blindfold you by the light they make.

The owl called from the naked-woman tree
As I came down by the Kyle farm to hear
Your house silent by the speaking sea.

I have come late but I have come before
Later with slaked steps from stone to stone
To hope to find you listening for the door.

I stand in the ticking room. My dear, I take
A moth kiss from your breath. The shore gulls cry.
I leave this at your ear for when you wake.

Keith
Douglas
(1920–1944)

Cairo Jag

Vergissmeinnicht

How to Kill

Keith Douglas is a man whose love of country and intelligent hunger for experience led him to enlist when the Second World War began, to fight, and to try to make sense of history from within its turbulence. Like the major British poets of the First World War, his art was tried and tempered by the experience, and then curtailed. When Douglas was killed in action the war was virtually over; he was twenty-four, a year younger than Owen at his death. Though young, he had a wide range of interests and of non-military experience. War and soldiering attracted him from childhood, but so did music, dance and literature. An instinct for manly experience combined with a love of creative activity.

Keith Castellain Douglas was born in Tunbridge Wells, an only child of an English father and a mother of French extraction. When he was eight, his father left. Douglas never saw him again. His childhood was solitary; he spent time drawing, beginning at the age of two to cover scraps of paper, floors, walls, any flat surface with his illustrations. A favourite childhood book was the *History of the Boer War*. There was unusual variety in his activities: the rugby player, the Officer Training Corps (OTC) trainee, the fine poet at the age of 14. He attended Christ's Hospital School in Sussex, then went up to Oxford in 1938. He edited a student newspaper and was active in amateur theatricals, usually backstage as designer.

In the army, Douglas served first in England, then in North Africa, where he courted action in the Desert Campaign. His prose book, *Alamein to Zem-Zem* is an outstanding account of his experience. He was injured by a land-mine and hospitalized briefly in Palestine, but soon returned to active service. He was killed in the Allied invasion of Normandy.

Small successes came early. At the age of 16 one of his poems was accepted for *New Verse*. Later his poems appeared in *Poetry London* and in minor anthologies. But he did little to advance his career and may have undervalued his talents. His *Collected Poems* (1951) appeared seven years after his death, but general recognition came only after Ted Hughes edited a *Selected Poems* (1964) and provided an introduction whose enthusiasm is well gauged. Hughes declares: 'He has invented a style that seems to be able to deal poetically with whatever it comes up against … It is a language for the whole mind, at its most wakeful, and in all situations.'

Impending death, which Douglas sensed as soon as he enlisted, is felt everywhere, always subtly. Charles Tomlinson writes, 'Death […] focuses rather than blurs the vision. Sensuous detail grows compact in its presence; life takes on an edge.' Douglas's best poems see death as a force within the object. Perhaps because of this sense of its inherence, unlike the other war poets Douglas is not an elegist. He accommodates subject matter on its own terms, not blurring it by sentiment or forcing extreme experience into an alien framework or tempering it with a poetic predisposition. A violent experience in the foreground is placed in a time context, where it occurs but is limited as experience by its context. Douglas identifies himself with all his characters and themes, with the poets of the First War, with the Jews, with the European predicament and with enemies and comrades.

He brings individual human situations up close; he exposes us by evoking his own exposure as calmly as language will allow. Hughes speaks of the 'air of improvisation' as 'a vital part' of Douglas's 'purity'.

Cairo Jag

Shall I get drunk or cut myself a piece of cake,
a pasty Syrian with a few words of English
or the Turk who says she is a princess – she dances
apparently by levitation? Or Marcelle, Parisienne
always preoccupied with her dull dead lover:
she has all the photographs and his letters
tied in a bundle and stamped *Décedé* in mauve ink.
All this takes place in a stink of jasmine.

But there are the streets dedicated to sleep
stenches and the sour smells, the sour cries
do not disturb their application to slumber
all day, scattered on the pavement like rags
afflicted with fatalism and hashish. The women
offering their children brown-paper breasts
dry and twisted, elongated like the skull,
Holbein's signature. But this stained white town
is something in accordance with mundane conventions–
Marcelle drops her Gallic airs and tragedy
suddenly shrieks in Arabic about the fare
with the cabman, links herself so
with the somnambulists and legless beggars:
it is all one, all as you have heard.

But by a day's travelling you reach a new world
the vegetation is of iron
dead tanks, gun barrels split like celery
the metal brambles have no flowers or berries
and there are all sorts of manure, you can imagine
the dead themselves, their boots, clothes and possessions
clinging to the ground, a man with no head
has a packet of chocolate and a souvenir of Tripoli.

dead tanks, gun barrels split
like celery

Vergissmeinnicht

Three weeks gone and the combatants gone
returning over the nightmare ground
we found the place again, and found
the soldier sprawling in the sun.

The frowning barrel of his gun
overshadowing. As we came on
that day, he hit my tank with one
like the entry of a demon.

Look. Here in the gunpit spoil
the dishonoured picture of his girl
who has put: *Steffi. Vergissmeinnicht.*
in a copybook gothic script.

We see him almost with content,
abased, and seeming to have paid
and mocked at by his own equipment
that's hard and good when he's decayed.

But she would weep to see today
how on his skin the swart flies move;
the dust upon the paper eye
and the burst stomach like a cave.

For here the lover and killer are mingled
who had one body and one heart.
And death who had the soldier singled
has done the lover mortal hurt.

> For here the
> lover and killer
> are mingled
> who had one
> body and one
> heart.

How to Kill

Under the parabola of a ball,
a child turning into a man,
I looked into the air too long.
The ball fell in my hand, it sang
in the closed fist: *Open Open*
Behold a gift designed to kill.

Now in my dial of glass appears
the soldier who is going to die.
He smiles, and moves about in ways
his mother knows, habits of his.
The wires touch his face: I cry
NOW. Death, like a familiar, hears

and look, has made a man of dust
of a man of flesh. This sorcery
I do. Being damned, I am amused
to see the centre of love diffused
and the waves of love travel into vacancy.
How easy it is to make a ghost.

The weightless mosquito touches
her tiny shadow on the stone,
and with how like, how infinite
a lightness, man and shadow meet.
They fuse. A shadow is a man
when the mosquito death approaches.

Edwin **Morgan**

(b. 1920)

A View of Things

Columba's Song

Siesta of a Hungarian Snake

Sir James Murray

Poetry, Edwin Morgan says, should 'acknowledge its environment'. His poetry also engages with history. He served in the Royal Army Medical Corps (1940–46), experienced Palestine and on his own terms he was part of that large moment in history. He was born in Glasgow. The Second World War broke his university education in two. At university before the war he read Eliot, Rimbaud (in French) and Mayakovsky (in Russian) and poetry opened up before him. What he learned later from the Beats, Williams and the Black Mountain poets was added, along with the work of the Brazilian Concrete Poets and the sound poems of Ernst Jandl.

He completed his degree in 1947, then taught in the English Department of the University of Glasgow until 1990. He became the Poet Laureate of Scotland in 2002. Even in his eighties he is versatile, with a sure control of traditional metrical and rhymed forms and a risk-taking inventiveness. He writes sonnets, ballads and elegies, dramatic monologues and epistles, but he has further claims as the arch-experimenter. Translations from a dozen languages, ancient and modern, opened his ears and eyes. He has been a concrete poet, a sound poet, a 'sci-fi' and 'video' poet; he has worked together with other writers and artists on collaborative projects.

Some regard him as too versatile, but the truth is that in a career spanning more than six decades poets can take a number of formal turns, invent, be versatile, and still revisit the more conventional terrain from which they have set off on quests. 'The Second Life' asks the question, 'Is it true that we come alive / not once, but many times?' The answer in his case must be 'yes' – even within a single book there are a dozen Morgans to deal with.

Insistently secular, at home in the present and hungry for the future, he finds occasions for poetry in the newspaper, on the radio, small incidents, 'what time barely kept'. He writes 'instamatic' poems, video poems, to capture and explore 'what actually happens'.

His first substantial book, *The Second Life*, appeared in 1968. Each poem was dated because it belonged to a specific time. The elegies were written soon after their subjects' deaths (Hemingway, Marilyn Monroe, Edith Piaf), the love poems soon after the incidents they evoke. A poem is anchored in its occasion. There is directness and candour about his love poems, integrated as they are into collections in which experiment, satire, elegy and other activities are going on. Nothing in Morgan, even the most amusing experiments, is 'merely literary'. Even the translations take English (or Scots) as close as it can go to the originals, getting at the creative dynamic itself.

Morgan is most often upbeat, committed to this world (for all its faults) because of its promise. The poems present dialogue, they believe in the social world. His is a salutary romanticism, rooted in the urban rather than the rural. Religion becomes a secular force, the foe is whoever says no to natural feeling, to growth and positive change.

A View of Things

what I love about dormice is their size
what I hate about rain is its sneer
what I love about the Bratach Gorm is its unflappability
what I hate about scent is its smell
what I love about newspapers is their etaoin shrdl
what I hate about philosophy is its pursed lip
what I love about Rory is his old grouse
what I hate about Pam is her pinkie
what I love about semi-precious stones is their preciousness
what I hate about diamonds is their mink
what I love about poetry is its ion engine
what I hate about hogs is their setae
what I love about love is its porridge-spoon
what I hate about hate is its eyes
what I love about hate is its salts
what I hate about love is its dog
what I love about Hank is his string vest
what I hate about the twins is their three gloves
what I love about Mabel is her teeter
what I hate about gooseberries is their look, feel, smell, and taste
what I love about the world is its shape
what I hate about a gun is its lock, stock, and barrel
what I love about bacon-and-eggs is its predictability
what I hate about derelict buildings is their reluctance to disintegrate
what I love about a cloud is its unpredictability
what I hate about you, chum, is your china
what I love about many waters is their inability to quench love

Columba's Song

Where's Brude? Where's Brude?
So many souls to be saved!
The bracken is thick, the wildcat is quick,
the foxes dance in the moonlight,
the salmon dance in the waters,
the adders dance in the thick brown bracken.
Where's Brude? Where's man?
There's too much nature here,
eagles and deer,
but where's the mind and where's the soul?
Show me your kings, your women, the man of the plough.
And cry me to your cradles.
It wasn't for a fox or an eagle I set sail!

Siesta of a Hungarian Snake

s sz sz SZ sz SZ sz ZS zs ZS zs zs z

Sir James Murray

I pick a daimen icker from the thrave
And chew it thoughtfully. I must be brave
And fight for this. My English colleagues frown
But words come skelpin rank and file, and down
They go, the kittle kimmers, they're well caught
And I won't give them up. Who would have thought
A gleg and gangrel Scot like me should barge,
Or rather breenge, like a kelpie at large
In the Cherwell, upon the very palladium
Of anglophilia? My sleekit radium
Is smuggled through the fluttering slips. My shed,
My outhouse with its thousand-plus well-fed
Pigeon-holes, has a northern exposure. Doon
Gaed stumpie in the ink all afternoon,
As Burns and I refreshed the dictionar
With cantrips from his dancing Carrick star!
O lovely words and lovely man! We'll caw
Before us yowes tae knowes; we'll shaw the braw
Auld baudrons by the ingle; we'll comb
Quotations to bring the wild whaup safely home.
Origin obscure? Origin uncertain? Origin unknown?
I love those eldritch pliskies that are thrown
At us from a too playful past, a store
Of splore we should never be blate to semaphore!
Oxford! here is a silent collieshangie
To spike your index-cards and keep them tangy.
Some, though not I, will jib at houghmagandy:
We'll maybe not get that past Mrs Grundy.
– But evening comes. To work, to work! To words!
The bats are turning into bauckie-birds.
The light in my scriptorium flickers gamely.
Pioneers must never labour tamely.
We steam along, we crawl, we pause, we hurtle,
And stir this English porridge with a spurtle.

A gleg and
gangrel
Scot like
me should
barge

Time Passing, Beloved

Time passing, and the memories of love
Coming back to me, carissima, no more mockingly
Than ever before; time passing, unslackening,
Unhastening, steadily; and no more
Bitterly, beloved, the memories of love
Coming into the shore.

How will it end? Time passing and our passages of love
As ever, beloved, blind
As ever before; time binding, unbinding
About us; and yet to remember
Never less chastening, nor the flame of love
Less like an ember.

What will become of us? Time
Passing, beloved, and we in a sealed
Assurance unassailed
By memory. How can it end,
This siege of a shore that no misgivings have steeled,
No doubts defend?

What will
become of us?
Time
Passing

Portland

after Pasternak

Portland, the Isle of Portland – how I love
Not the place, its name! It is as if
These names were your name, and the cliff, the breaking
Of waves along a reach of tumbled stone
Were a configuration of your own
Firm slopes and curves – your clavicles, your shoulder.
A glimpse of that can set the hallway shaking.
And I am a night sky that is tired of shining,
Tired of its own hard brilliance, and I sink.

Tomorrow morning, grateful, I shall seem
Keen, but be less clear-headed than I think;
A brightness more than clarity will sail
Off lips that vapour formulations, make
Clear sound, full rhyme, and rational order take
Account of a dream, a sighing cry, a moan,

Like foam on all three sides at midnight lighting
Up, far off, a seaward jut of stone.

Aubade

I wish for you that when you wake
You emulate the leaf and bird;
That like them, touched with grace, you take
Note of the wind. You have not heard
Its low-voiced billows yet, nor seen
(Lost in your less elated rest)
The empty light upon the green,
The leaves and tumbling birds that gave
The wind its due, and then redressed
That small excess, each bounding spray
A boat that dances on the wave,
A whip that tingles in the day.

Their Rectitude Their Beauty

'The angels rejoice in
the excellencies of God;
the inferior creatures in
His goodness; sinners only
in His forgiveness.'

His polar oppositions;
the habitable zones,
His clemencies; and
His smiling divagations,
uncovenanted mercies,

who turned the hard rock into a standing water
and the flint-stone into a springing well.

The voice of joy and health is in the dwellings of the righteous;
my eyes are running with rheum
from looking for that health

in one who has stuck by
His testimonies;
who has delighted in
His regimen; who has run
the circuit of His requirements;
whose songs in the caravanserai
have been about His statutes,

not to deserve nor observe them
(having done neither) but
for the angelic reason:

their rectitude,
their beauty.

who turned the
hard rock into a
standing water

Philip
Larkin
(1922–1985)

Deceptions

Almost every poem that Philip Larkin included in the four books published during his lifetime was assiduously complete. Seldom does he miss a target; the lapses in diction are usually deliberate. He of all the 'movement' poets remained true to his point of departure, and only he of his generation achieved the large readership which other poets desired. He did as much as Housman to turn back the clock of English poetry; like Housman, he is a modern poet often quoted – in church, in parliament, in the classroom – by people who latch on to a phrase or stanza without exploring what the poem as a whole might mean.

He was born into the conservative middle class, with a father whose 'little Englandism' was extreme, with a quiet, undemonstrative mother to whom he was devoted. He attended Grammar school in Coventry – a solitary adolescence filled with novel writing as other boys' is with football. Manuscripts were disposed of furtively. From there he went to St John's College, Oxford. He was infatuated with Dylan Thomas's poems and with Yeats up to *Words for Music Perhaps*. Hardy was his tonic against the excesses of Bohemia. Auden provided a crucial vaccination against Romanticism. He became a librarian in Ireland, then in Leeds and finally at Hull University.

He does not idealize the past. He does not see it, in Hardy's terms, as unrealized, either. It is simply unrealizable. Not Wordsworth's infant trailing clouds of glory behind whom gates of the prison house close; not Browning's 'Never the time and the place / And the loved ones all together' or even Hardy's 'Everything glowed with a gleam / But we were looking – away'. Death is Larkin's abiding muse, not love or even lust with its temporary solaces.

Larkin's inverted Romanticism means that he distrusts the subjective, his own and that of the characters he creates and the people he observes. He evokes them through the physical objects with which they surround themselves. The 'cut price crowd' rushes from stark new suburbs to shop, its values determined and defined by the objects it rushes to acquire.

'I never think of poetry or the poetry scene, only separate poems written by individuals,' he says. His task as a poet is 'to preserve things I have seen/thought/felt'; poems are 'verbal devices', 'verbal pickling'. They build towards a point of 'lift-off ': poems are structured, then, to a thematic or dramatic climax which can occur in the release of an image or a change in tone from the ironic and light-hearted to deadly earnest. The poems are subtly made and self-contained – we respond without footnotes, without consulting any document beyond a daily paper. They are replete with the small dramas, losses and frustrations which add up to the large gradual tragedy of lives in a thousand furnished rooms and modest houses, in a particular country at a particular time.

Why is a poet of such negative temper so popular? Perhaps most of all because of the insidiousness of his verse – the way that after one or two readings it lodges in memory. It has, with its characteristic details, its spoken tones, its formal assurance, the rhythm or pitch of truth, and a poet who speaks bleak seeming-truths is probably more valuable than one who provides airy consolations. The candour of Larkin is different in kind from the candour of Robert Lowell – not more English precisely, but more democratic. His truths (if they are true) carry at least the consolation of clarity, unblurred by dark autobiographical resentments. No doubt they are there behind the poems, but the poet has had the tact to push them very nearly out of sight.

Deceptions

'Of course I was drugged, and so heavily I did not regain my consciousness until the next morning. I was horrified to discover that I had been ruined, and for some days I was inconsolable, and cried like a child to be killed or sent back to my aunt.'

– Mayhew, *London Labour and the London Poor*

Even so distant, I can taste the grief,
Bitter and sharp with stalks, he made you gulp.
The sun's occasional print, the brisk brief
Worry of wheels along the street outside
Where bridal London bows the other way,
And light, unanswerable and tall and wide,
Forbids the scar to heal, and drives
Shame out of hiding. All the unhurried day,
Your mind lay open like a drawer of knives.

Slums, years, have buried you. I would not dare
Console you if I could. What can be said,
Except that suffering is exact, but where
Desire takes charge, readings will grow erratic?
For you would hardly care
That you were less deceived, out on that bed,
Than he was, stumbling up the breathless stair
To burst into fulfilment's desolate attic.

The Trees

The trees are coming into leaf
Like something almost being said;
The recent buds relax and spread,
Their greenness is a kind of grief.

Is it that they are born again
And we grow old? No, they die too.
Their yearly trick of looking new
Is written down in rings of grain.

Yet still the unresting castles thresh
In fullgrown thickness every May.
Last year is dead, they seem to say,
Begin afresh, afresh, afresh.

MCMXIV

Those long uneven lines
Standing as patiently
As if they were stretched outside
The Oval or Villa Park,
The crowns of hats, the sun
On moustached archaic faces
Grinning as if it were all
An August Bank Holiday lark;

And the shut shops, the bleached
Established names on the sunblinds,
The farthings and sovereigns,
And dark-clothed children at play
Called after kings and queens,
The tin advertisements
For cocoa and twist, and the pubs
Wide open all day;

And the countryside not caring
The place-names all hazed over
With flowering grasses, and fields
Shadowing Domesday lines
Under wheat's restless silence;
The differently-dressed servants
With tiny rooms in huge houses,
The dust behind limousines;

Never such innocence,
Never before or since,
As changed itself to past
Without a word – the men
Leaving the gardens tidy,
The thousands of marriages
Lasting a little while longer:
Never such innocence again.

Ambulances

Closed like confessionals, they thread
Loud noons of cities, giving back
None of the glances they absorb.
Light glossy grey, arms on a plaque,
They come to rest at any kerb:
All streets in time are visited.

Then children strewn on steps or road,
Or women coming from the shops
Past smells of different dinners, see
A wild white face that overtops
Red stretcher-blankets momently
As it is carried in and stowed,

And sense the solving emptiness
That lies just under all we do,
And for a second get it whole,
So permanent and blank and true.
The fastened doors recede. *Poor soul,*
They whisper at their own distress;

For borne away in deadened air
May go the sudden shut of loss
Round something nearly at an end,
And what cohered in it across
The years, the unique random blend
Of families and fashions, there

At last begin to loosen. Far
From the exchange of love to lie
Unreachable inside a room
The traffic parts to let go by
Brings closer what is left to come,
And dulls to distance all we are.

James
K.Baxter

(1926–1972)

Morning and Evening Calm

From Jerusalem Sonnets, Sonnet 36

Haere Ra

Moss on plum branches …

A pair of sandals …

The New Zealand poet James K. Baxter died at the age of 46, with over 600 pages of *Collected Poems* (1979) in a volume that excluded his more ephemeral writings. One of the most precocious poets of the last century, he has gradually found a readership beyond New Zealand, but even now his stature is not fully acknowledged. The poetry, damaged by his serious alcoholism and much of the later work written with the assistance of drugs, is uneven, but the best writing, some of it from the darkest periods, can be called 'major'.

In a lecture he recalls how he wrote his first poem. 'I climbed up to a hole in a bank in a hill above the sea, and there fell into the attitude of *listening* out of which poems may rise – not to the sound of the sea, but to the unheard sound of which poems are translations – it was then that I first endured that intense effort of *listening*, like a man chained to the ground trying to stand upright and walk – and from this intensity of listening the words emerged –'. He was seven years old. 'I don't think my methods of composition have changed much since that time. The daimon has always to be invoked; and there is no certainty that he will answer the invitation.' His first book was published when he was 18.

Baxter embodies contradictions: a patriot, savage about his native land; a Roman Catholic asserting independence within the church and breaking its rules and institutions; a missionary to the Maoris who sentimentalized and half-adopted their culture; a father who watched his children inject drugs.

His father, an Otago farmer who educated himself, was a pacifist during the First World War. His mother, the daughter of a professor of English and classics, herself educated at Newnham College, Cambridge, encouraged her son to write. When he was 11 the family went to Europe for two years and he returned ill at ease with the New Zealand world. When he went to university in Otago at the age of 17, he fell into heavy drinking. He dropped out, took odd jobs, tried again at university and eventually took a BA. In 1958 he travelled to India and Japan, saw the poor, and began the long march of conscience towards his conversion to Catholicism and to Jerusalem, the religious house he established in 1968 and where he became the unanointed guru.

He certainly found models abroad. He drew on Dylan Thomas and Yeats, and on some of his American contemporaries, notably Lowell whose *Life Studies* affected him. *The Jerusalem Sonnets* (1970), written shortly after he became the leader of his community, mark a high point of candour and originality, in his language, his forms and his human vision.

Why did Baxter write so much? His is not the casual copiousness of the Beats or Frank O'Hara; he is not effusive or 'spontaneous'. He revised his poems. He worked hard at them and there is progression, and yet a final thinness of subject, as though the language exceeds its occasions two-to-one. Though Baxter was not a beatnik, in a different world he might have been; a world with men of Burroughs's and Kerouac's anarchy might have directed his talent and energy into formal innovation. Baxter does not quite 'make it new'; he does not make it consistently real, either. The success is huge and rhetorical, the shortcomings intimate and formal, until the very last poems ('Moss on plum branches' and 'A pair of sandals'), scrawled down as he made his way out of the world.

Morning and Evening Calm

Morning and evening calm: the Lord has spoken
from no devouring whirlwind, but the still
green garden of a world-sustaining Will.
O tenderly by Him the heart is broken,

and Bartimaeus finds in the All-Seeing
his eyes again, grown younger for his pains:
while disparate Love, that else were iron grains
draws meaning from the magnet of His Being.

He has denied my sorrow and my hunger
with voice of wounds, and bleeding I reply
that am content in Him to crave no longer

(dovelike and calm the overarching sky);
and love of flesh to flesh itself shall die
His terrible Compassion being stronger.

From Jerusalem Sonnets, Sonnet 36

Brother Ass, Brother Ass, you are full of fancies,
You want this and that – a woman, a thistle,

A poem, a coffeebreak, a white bed, no crabs;
And now you complain of the weight of the Rider

Who will set you free to gallop in the light of the sun!
Ah well, kick Him off then, and see how you go

Lame-footed in the brambles; your disconsolate bray
Is ugly in my ears – long ago, long ago,

The battle was fought and the issue decided
As to who would be King – go on, little donkey

Saddled and bridled by the Master of the world,
Be glad you can distinguish not an inch of the track,

That the stones are sharp, that your hide can itch,
That His true weight is heavy on your back.

Saddled and bridled
by the Master of the world

Haere Ra

Farewell to Hiruharama –
The green hills and the river fog
Cradling the convent and the Maori houses –

The peach tree at my door is broken, sister,
It carried too much fruit,
It hangs now by a bent strip of bark –

But better that way than the grey moss
Cloaking the branch like an old man's beard;
We are broken by the Love of the Many

And then we are at peace
Like the fog, like the river, like a roofless house
That lets the sun stream in because it cannot help it.

> We are
> broken by
> the Love of
> the Many

Moss on plum branches ...

Moss on plum branches and
A soft rain falling – no other house
Spread out its arms around me
As this has done – I go
From here with a gap inside me where a world
Has been plucked from my entrails – fire and
Food, flowers and faces
Painted on walls – the voices of two friends
Recalling the always present paradise
We enter and cannot remain in.

A pair of sandals ...

A pair of sandals, old black pants
And leather coat – I must go, my friends,
Into the dark, the cold, the first beginning
Where the ribs of the ancestor are the rafters
Of a meeting house – windows broken
And the floor white with bird dung – in there
The ghosts gather who will instruct me
And when the river fog rises
Te ra rite tonu te Atua –
The sun who is like the Lord
Will warm my bones, and his arrows
Will pierce to the centre of the shapeless clay of the mind.

Allen
Ginsberg
(1926–1997)

From *Kaddish (I)*

'I want to be known as the most brilliant man in America,' Allen Ginsberg said in 'Ego Confession'. He also wrote poems. 'His poetry made things happen,' an obituary declared. That's not quite right. His performances and polemics did. His example as a performer touched poets remote from him in temperament like Robert Lowell and Bob Dylan. But the poems as texts on a page have a half-existence without his voice pushing them. The texts are, more than any of the other poetry in this book, scores keen to escape into the air as recitation – as song.

He was born in Paterson, New Jersey, his father a poet and teacher, his mother a woman who suffered from mental illness. The presence of his father at once inspired and inhibited his development. When he wrote 'Howl' he dreaded not the censor but his father's response to the lines 'who let themselves be fucked in the ass by saintly motorcyclists, and screamed with joy, / who blew and were blown by those human seraphim, the sailors, caresses of Atlantic and Caribbean love, / who balled in the morning in the evenings in rosegardens and the grass of public parks and cemeteries scattering their semen freely to whomever come who may' and so on. Once he had got this into print, he had broken a personal taboo and could say anything he liked.

Ginsberg studied at Columbia University. He dropped out for a year, travelling and doing odd jobs. Wandering became a vocation. The reading tour was a way of life, a heroic progress around the globe again and again. He was the high priest of the Beats, and he spread the word. His most celebrated stopover was in Prague where, in 1965, students elected him King of the May and he was immediately deported. He wrote 'Kral Majales' to commemorate this martyrdom at the hands of 'the Marxists' who 'have beat me upon the street'.

Those who experienced Ginsberg's readings in the first three decades of his performing life know how much he was a *body*, whose mission seemed to be to deliver the audience back to a sense of its bodies individually and its body collectively, the physical being an instrument of exploration and of praise. 'Everything is holy! everybody's holy! everywhere is holy! everyday is in eternity! Everyman's an angel!' When the prophet departed, the audience was left clutching the book. In his absence, what residual magic did the poems have?

We can follow Ginsberg through three identities. First is the young poet struggling under the constraining patronage of William Carlos Williams, but with the soulful spirit already bubbling away in him. Then there is the Ginsberg (a friend of William Burroughs and Jack Kerouac) visited by the spirit William Blake in the privacy of his room. In the wake of these visitations came the poems 'Howl' and later 'Kaddish'. Then, travelling on a Japanese train, he became Allen Ginsberg III: a Buddhist no longer burning towards death but celebrating life (through his own) in all its wholeness. A gentler poet, American still, ambitious and – when need be – playing to the gallery.

Ginsberg dropped on American poetry like a bomb; his generation outgrew him and American poetry has outgrown him, but the legend lives and 'Howl', 'Kaddish' and other poems still shout and whisper. Adrienne Rich, a more profound and consistent radical, redefines the spaces that English language poetry can occupy and develop. Ginsberg's is poetry of powerful but local revolt.

From Kaddish (I)

For Naomi Ginsberg, 1894–1956

Strange now to think of you, gone without corsets & eyes, while I walk on
   the sunny pavement of Greenwich Village,
downtown Manhattan, clear winter noon, and I've been up all night, talking,
   talking, reading the Kaddish aloud, listening to Ray Charles blues
   shout blind on the phonograph
the rhythm the rhythm—and your memory in my head three years after—And
   read Adonais' last triumphant stanzas aloud—wept, realizing how we suffer—
And how Death is that remedy all singers dream of, sing, remember,
   prophesy as in the Hebrew Anthem, or the Buddhist Book of Answers—and
   my own imagination of a withered leaf—at dawn—
Dreaming back thru life, Your time—and mine accelerating toward
   Apocalypse,
the final moment—the flower burning in the Day—and what comes after,
looking back on the mind itself that saw an Amerian city
a flash away, and the great dream of Me or China, or you and a phantom
   Russia, or a crumpled bed that never existed—
like a poem in the dark—escaped back to Oblivion—
No more to say, and nothing to weep for but the Beings in the Dream,
   trapped in its disappearance,
sighing, screaming with it, buying and selling pieces of phantom, worship-
   ping each other,
worshipping the God included in it all—longing or inevitability?—while it
   lasts, a Vision—anything more?
It leaps about me, as I go out and walk the street, look back over my shoulder,
   Seventh Avenue, the battlements of window office buildings shouldering
   each other high, under a cloud, tall as the sky an instant—and the sky
   above—an old blue place.
or down the Avenue to the south, to—as I walk toward the Lower East Side
   —where you walked 50 years ago, little girl—from Russia, eating the
   first poisonous tomatoes of America—frightened on the dock—
then struggling in the crowds of Orchard Street toward what?—toward
   Newark—
toward candy store, first home-made sodas of the century, hand-churned ice
   cream in backroom on musty brownfloor boards—
Toward education marriage nervous breakdown, operation, teaching school,
   and learning to be mad, in a dream—what is this life?
Toward the Key in the window—and the great Key lays its head of light
   on top of Manhattan, and over the floor, and lays down on the
   sidewalk—in a single vast beam, moving, as I walk down First toward
   the Yiddish Theater—and the place of poverty
you knew, and I know, but without caring now—Strange to have moved
   thru Paterson, and the West, and Europe and here again,
with the cries of Spaniards now in the doorstops doors and dark boys on
   the street, fire escapes old as you
—Tho you're not old now, that's left here with me—
Myself, anyhow, maybe as old as the universe—and I guess that dies with us—
   enough to cancel all that comes—What came is gone forever every time—

That's good! That leaves it open for no regret—no fear radiators, lacklove,
  torture even toothache in the end—
Though while it comes it is a lion that eats the soul–and the lamb, the soul,
  in us, alas, offering itself in sacrifice to change's fierce hunger—hair
  and teeth—and the roar of bonepain, skull bare, break rib, rot-skin,
  braintricked Implacability.
Ai! ai! we do worse! We are in a fix! And you're out, Death let you out,
  Death had the Mercy, you're done with your century, done with God, done
  with the path thru it—Done with yourself at last—Pure—Back to the Babe
  dark before your Father, before us all—before the world—
There, rest. No more suffering for you. I know where you've gone, it's good.
No more flowers in the summer fields of New York, no joy now, no more
  fear of Louis,
and no more of his sweetness and glasses, his high school decades, debts,
  loves, frightened telephone calls, conception beds, relatives, hands—
No more of sister Elanor,—she gone before you—we kept it secret you
  killed her—or she killed herself to bear with you—an arthritic heart
  —But Death's killed you both—No matter—
Nor your memory of your mother, 1915 tears in silent movies weeks and
  weeks—forgetting, aggrieve watching Marie Dressler address human-
  ity, Chaplin dance in youth,
or Boris Godunov, Chaliapin's at the Met, halling his voice of a weeping Czar
  —by standing room with Elanor & Max—watching also the Capitalists take
  seats in Orchestra, white furs, diamonds,
with the YPSL's hitch-hiking thru Pennsylvania, in black baggy gym skirts
  pants, photograph of 4 girls holding each other round the waste, and
  laughing eye, too coy, virginal solitude of 1920
all girls grown old, or dead, now, and that long hair in the grave—lucky to
  have husbands later—
You made it—I came too—Eugene my brother before (still grieving now and
  will gream on to his last stiff hand, as he goes thru his cancer—or kill
  —later perhaps—soon he will think—)
And it's the last moment I remember, which I see them all, thru myself, now
  —tho not you
I didn't foresee what you felt—what more hideous gape of bad mouth came
  first—to you—and were you prepared?
To go where? In that Dark—that—in that God? a radiance? A Lord in the
  Void? Like an eye in the black cloud in a dream? Adonoi at last, with you?
Beyond my remembrance! Incapable to guess! Not merely the yellow skull
  in the grave, or a box of worm dust, and a stained ribbon—Deaths-
  head with Halo? can you believe it?
Is it only the sun that shines once for the mind, only the flash of existence,
  than none ever was?
Nothing beyond what we have—what you had—that so pitiful—yet Triumph,
to have been here, and changed, like a tree, broken, or flower—fed to the
  ground—but mad, with its petals, colored, thinking Great Universe,
  shaken, cut in the head, leaf strip, hid in an egg crate hospital, cloth
  wrapped, sore—freaked in the moon brain, Naughtless. [...]

Frank
O'Hara
(1926–1966)

Autobiographia Literaria

Why I am not a Painter

The Day Lady Died

At Harvard, John Ashbery says, Frank O'Hara 'had a very sort of pugnacious and pugilistic look. He had a broken nose. He didn't look like a very cordial person.' Ashbery got to know him properly a month before graduation. They became friends in New York.

Many people tend to get O'Hara wrong, as a man and as a poet. He was born in Baltimore, Maryland, and raised in Grafton, Massachusetts. He served in the navy for two years, then went to Harvard where he took a degree in Music. After graduate school, in 1951 he settled in New York and took a job with the Museum of Modern Art. His life became New York and the art scene of the time – Willem De Kooning, Franz Kline and Jackson Pollock – the abstract expressionists. He was an editorial associate of *Art News*. In 1960 he became assistant curator of the Museum of Modern Art. He was killed on Fire Island in an accident with a beach buggy, struck down in the early hours of 24 July 1966 in the dark on the dunes.

He was casual about his poems: it's not that he didn't value them, but he didn't worry much about them after they were complete. He could be scrupulous but was not always too concerned about the final text. The editor of the posthumous *Collected Poems* found more than 500 (others have been added since), many previously unpublished. What mattered to O'Hara was the writing of them. He published only four collections, none of them with 'leading' publishing houses. He preferred to work with galleries, as though the poems were entries in an exhibition catalogue – an exhibition made of daily life.

In 'Notes on *Second Avenue*', appended to his longest and most ambitious poem, he rejects theories of poetry: 'I have a feeling that the philosophical reduction of reality to a dealable-with system so distorts life that one's "reward" for the endeavor (a minor one at that) is illness both from inside and from outside.' His poems are busy in the world; they have no inclination to stand back and preach or to invent monstrous forms.

He is the most New York of the New York poets. He experiments with prose poems, mixtures of prose and verse, complicating formal choices, with Williamsesque lineation here, a touch of Auden there where he experiments with sonnets, or ridicules Wyatt, or apostrophizes friends, or celebrates. There is Jane Freilicher, whom he watches as a painter would watch his models and portrays in a hundred postures and gestures. At no point does he disguise his sexual imagination. He doesn't foreground it, either.

The characters in his city are poets, painters, editors, arts administrators, delicatessen people and booksellers. He calls God 'The Finger' and has dubious and riotous thoughts about him. As he develops, the poems experiment with 'painterly' approaches, the cubism of language. He reifies language. Words fit things and periods and attitudes, and it is getting that fit, for descriptive or ironic purposes, that interests O'Hara. There are grand poems about big and little themes, lightly ironized, and then the larger ironies of the mature work, where heartbreak and laughter hold hands.

'Pain always produces logic, which is very bad for you', O'Hara warns us. Authority produces logic, too, perhaps because it produces pain. And logic is invariably reductive and constraining, leading to rules and programmes and building the prison house. 'I'm not saying that I don't have practically the most lofty ideas of anyone writing today, but what difference does that make? They're just ideas.'

Autobiographia Literaria

When I was a child
I played by myself in a
corner of the schoolyard
all alone.

I hated dolls and I
hated games, animals were
not friendly and birds
flew away.

If anyone was looking
for me I hid behind a
tree and cried out 'I am
an orphan.'

And here I am, the
center of all beauty!
writing these poems!
Imagine!

> If anyone was looking
> for me I hid behind a
> tree and cried out 'I am
> an orphan.'

Why I am not a Painter

I am not a painter, I am a poet.
Why? I think I would rather be
a painter, but I am not. Well,

for instance, Mike Goldberg
is starting a painting. I drop in.
'Sit down and have a drink' he
says. I drink; we drink. I look
up. 'You have SARDINES in it.'
'Yes, it needed something there.'
'Oh.' I go and the days go by
and I drop in again. The painting
is going on, and I go, and the days
go by. I drop in. The painting is
finished. 'Where's SARDINES?'
All that's left is just
letters, 'It was too much,' Mike says.

But me? One day I am thinking of
a color: orange. I write a line
about orange. Pretty soon it is a
whole page of words, not lines.

Then another page. There should be
so much more, not of orange, of
words, of how terrible orange is
and life. Days go by. It is even in
prose, I am a real poet. My poem
is finished and I haven't mentioned
orange yet. It's twelve poems, I call
it ORANGES. And one day in a gallery
I see Mike's painting, called SARDINES.

The Day Lady Died

It is 12:20 in New York a Friday
three days after Bastille day, yes
it is 1959 and I go get a shoeshine
because I will get off the 4:19 in Easthampton
at 7:15 and then go straight to dinner
and I don't know the people who will feed me

I walk up the muggy street beginning to sun
and have a hamburger and a malted and buy
an ugly NEW WORLD WRITING to see what the poets
in Ghana are doing these days
                              I go on to the bank
and Miss Stillwagon (first name Linda I once heard)
doesn't even look up my balance for once in her life
and in the GOLDEN GRIFFIN I get a little Verlaine
for Patsy with drawings by Bonnard although I do
think of Hesiod, trans. Richmond Lattimore or
Brendan Behan's new play or Le Balcon or Les Nègres
of Genet, but I don't, I stick with Verlaine
after practically going to sleep with quandariness

and for Mike I just stroll into the PARK LANE
Liquor Store and ask for a bottle of Strega and
then I go back where I came from to 6th Avenue
and the tobacconist in the Ziegfeld Theatre and
casually ask for a carton of Gauloises and a carton
of Picayunes, and a NEW YORK POST with her face on it

and I am sweating a lot by now and thinking of
leaning on the john door in the 5 SPOT
while she whispered a song along the keyboard
to Mal Waldron and everyone and I stopped breathing

Some Trees

These are amazing: each
Joining a neighbor, as though speech
Were a still performance.
Arranging by chance

To meet as far this morning
From the world as agreeing
With it, you and I
Are suddenly what the trees try

To tell us we are:
That their merely being there
Means something; that soon
We may touch, love, explain.

And glad not to have invented
Such comeliness, we are surrounded:
A silence already filled with noises,
A canvas on which emerges

A chorus of smiles, a winter morning.
Placed in a puzzling light, and moving,
Our days put on such reticence
These accents seem their own defense.

That their merely being there Means something

What is Poetry

The medieval town, with frieze
Of boy scouts from Nagoya? The snow

That came when we wanted it to snow?
Beautiful images? Trying to avoid

Ideas, as in this poem? But we
Go back to them as to a wife, leaving

The mistress we desire? Now they
Will have to believe it

As we believe it. In school
All the thought got combed out:

What was left was like a field.
Shut your eyes, and you can feel it for miles around.

Now open them on a thin vertical path.
It might give us—what?—some flowers soon?

For John Clare

Kind of empty in the way it sees everything, the earth gets to its feet and salutes the sky. More of a success at it this time than most others it is. The feeling that the sky might be in the back of someone's mind. Then there is no telling how many there are. They grace everything—bush and tree—to take the roisterer's mind off his caroling—so it's like a smooth switch back. To what was aired in their previous conniption fit. There is so much to be seen everywhere that it's like not getting used to it, only there is so much it never feels new, never any different. You are standing looking at that building and you cannot take it all in, certain details are already hazy and the mind boggles. What will it all be like in five years' time when you try to remember?

Will there have been boards in between the grass part and the edge of the street? As long as that couple is stopping to look in that window over there we cannot go. We feel like they have to tell us we can, but they never look our way and they are already gone, gone far into the future—the night of time. If we could look at a photograph of it and say there they are, they never really stopped but there they are. There is so much to be said, and on the surface of it very little gets said.

There ought to be room for more things, for a spreading out, like. Being immersed in the details of rock and field and slope—letting them come to you for once, and then meeting them halfway would be so much easier—if they took an ingenuous pride in being in one's blood. Alas, we perceive them if at all as those things that were meant to be put aside—costumes of the supporting actors or voice trilling at the end of a narrow enclosed street. You can do nothing with them. Not even offer to pay.

It is possible that finally, like coming to the end of a long, barely perceptible rise, there is mutual cohesion and interaction. The whole scene is fixed in your mind, the music all present, as though you could see each note as well as hear it. I say this because there is an uneasiness in things just now. Waiting for something to be over before you are forced to notice it. The pollarded trees scarcely bucking the wind—and yet it's keen, it makes you fall over. Clabbered sky. Seasons that pass with a rush. After all it's their time too—nothing says they aren't to make something of it. As for Jenny Wren, she cares, hopping about on her little twig like she was tryin' to tell us somethin', but that's just it, she couldn't even if she wanted to—dumb bird. But the others—and they in some way must know too—it would never occur to them to want to, even if they could take the first step of the terrible journey toward feeling somebody should act, that ends in utter confusion and hopelessness, east of the sun and west of the moon. So their comment is: 'No comment.' Meanwhile the whole history of probabilities is coming to life, starting in the upper left-hand corner, like a sail.

There is so much to be said, and on the surface of it very little gets said.

At North Farm

Somewhere someone is traveling furiously toward you,
At incredible speed, traveling day and night,
Through blizzards and desert heat, across torrents, through narrow passes.
But will he know where to find you,
Recognize you when he sees you,
Give you the thing he has for you?

Hardly anything grows here,
Yet the granaries are bursting with meal,
The sacks of meal piled to the rafters.
The streams run with sweetness, fattening fish;
Birds darken the sky. Is it enough
That the dish of milk is set out at night,
That we think of him sometimes,
Sometimes and always, with mixed feelings?

Just Walking Around

What name do I have for you?
Certainly there is no name for you
In the sense that the stars have names
That somehow fit them. Just walking around,

An object of curiosity to some,
But you are too preoccupied
By the secret smudge in the back of your soul
To say much, and wander around,

Smiling to yourself and others.
It gets to be kind of lonely
But at the same time off-putting,
Counterproductive, as you realize once again

That the longest way is the most efficient way,
The one that looped among islands, and
You always seemed to be traveling in a circle.
And now that the end is near

The segments of the trip swing open like an orange.
There is light in there, and mystery and food.
Come see it. Come not for me but it.
But if I am still there, grant that we may see each other.

What is written …

What is written on the paper
on the table by the bed? Is there something there
or was that from another last night?

Why is that bird ignoring us,
pausing in mid-flight, to take another direction?
Is it feelings of guilt about the spool
it dropped on the bank of a stream,
into which it eventually rolled? Dark spool,
moving oceanward now – what other fate could have been yours?
You could have lived in a drawer
for many years, imprisoned, a ward of the state. Now you are free
to call the shots pretty much as they come.
Poor, bald thing.

> Why is that bird ignoring us,
> pausing in mid-flight, to take
> another direction?

Annuals and Perennials

Telling it so simple, so far away,
as this America, home of the free,
colored ashes smeared on the base
or pedestal that flourishes ways of doubting
to be graceful, wave a slender hand…

We are fleet and persecuting
as hawks or crows.
We suffer for the lies we told, not wanting to
yet cupped in the wristlock of grace,
teenage Borgias or Gonzagas,
gold against gray in bands streaming,
meaning no harm, we never

meant it to, this stream that outpours now
haplessly into the vestibule that awaits.

We have shapes but no power.

Thomas
Kinsella
(b. 1928)

Soft, to Your Places

The Laundress

A Portrait of the Artist

In the late 1960s, the best-known Irish poet of the newer generation was Thomas Kinsella, whose volume *Nightwalker and Other Poems* (1968) was widely admired, if not then understood. In 1972 *Butcher's Dozen: A Lesson for the Octave of Widgery* appeared, a response to Bloody Sunday (the killings in Northern Ireland by British troops) and to the Widgery Inquiry which tried to settle the matter. That impassioned, effective and far from conciliatory poem – eighteenth-century in mode – contributed to Kinsella's eclipse in Britain.

Kinsella knew his Auden well when he began writing. Even the poems he wrote in the 1950s were enlarged by his understanding of the ambitious forms and themes of the by then American poet. It was never a question of imitation, rather of transposition. Kinsella is an Irish poet through and through. His translations from the Irish tradition are a key resource. Ireland for him implies Swift and Goldsmith, Mangan, Davis and Fergusson, and pre-eminently Yeats.

He swims naturally and resolutely against tides of fashion. He does not go in fear of abstractions, but he gives them body and valency. He is also alive to place, to character and voice; he is alive to direct and oblique narrative. He is alive to politics. He developed allegories ('emblematic' or 'heraldic' verse, Donald Davie calls it) in *Nightwalker*; and when he began to read Ezra Pound his poetry found its own prosody. Audenesque habits of eloquent closure are fused with a prosody inferred from Pound, making his mature poems some of the most remarkable in modern English-language poetry.

Born in modest circumstances in Dublin, Kinsella is not a child of the fields or suburbs but of the city. He abandoned a science degree at University College Dublin and was a civil servant until 1965. He became a professor at universities in the United States, a director of the Kuala and Dolmen Presses, and founded his own Peppercanister Press through which his poems and sequences were first published, before being gathered together and issued in longer volumes. The Peppercanister books build towards a major single work, and we are put in mind, though Kinsella does not invite us to do so, of Pound's *Cantos*. The patterns we begin to discern and the geographies which build on Dublin in its different phases are difficult and fascinating. The poems are a gathering together, with history, personal candour, polemic and argument.

Kinsella describes a 'Dual Tradition' in Irish literature, attempting to bring back fully into play the Irish linguistic tradition and the poets of Ireland neglected during centuries of English domination. The challenge is to recover rather than invent a language, to live rather than exist a life.

> Better is an handful with quietness
> than both hands full
> with travail and vexation of spirit.

> Better to leave now, and no more of this loving upset,
> hate staining the door-jamb from a head possessed
> – all things settled sour in their place,
> my blind fingers forsaking your face.

> Yet worst is the fool that foldeth his hands
> and eateth his own flesh

Soft, to Your Places

Soft, to your places, animals.
Your legendary duty calls.
It is, to be
Lucky for my love and me
And yet we have seen that all's
A fiction that is heard of love's difficulty.

And what if the simple primrose show
That mighty work went on below
Before it grew
A moral miracle for us two?
Since of ourselves we know
Beauty to be an easy thing, this will do.

But O when beauty's brought to pass
Will Time set down his hour-glass
And rest content,
His hand upon that monument?
Unless it is so, alas
That the heart's calling is but to go naked and diffident.

Soft, to your places, love; I kiss
Because it is, because it is.

> That the heart's calling is but to go naked and diffident.

The Laundress

Her chair drawn to the door,
A basket at her feet,
She sat against the sun
And stitched a linen sheet.
Over harrowed Flanders
August moved the wheat.

Poplars sharing the wind
With Saxony and France
Dreamed at her gate,
Soared in a Summer trance.
A cluck in the cobbled yard:
A shadow changed its stance.

As a fish disturbs the pond
And sinks without a stain
The heels of ripeness fluttered

Under her apron. Then
Her heart grew strained and light
As the shell that shields the grain.

Bluntly through the doorway
She stared at shed and farm,
At yellow fields unstitching
About the hoarded germ,
At land that would spread white
When she had reached her term.

The sower plumps his acre,
Flanders turns to the heat,
The winds of Heaven winnow
And the wheels grind the wheat.
She searched in her basket
And fixed her ruffled sheet.

A Portrait of the Artist

We might have guessed it would end in argument
and the personal. The cool, acid exchanges
in the small hours, hoarse in the hall:
An architect is an artist! His first duty is beauty!
Finding our way down the steps;
walking up the terrace in relief.

*

A pair of figures the other side of the Canal.

*They had reached the canal bridge
and, turning from their course ...*
continued, locked in argument.

       About there.

One, nagging beauty to her place
among the senses. And the fool
lending a quick, inadequate ear:

      But what is beauty.

A jewel of process.
The fugitive held fast, exact in its accident

My hands framed your throat in the night air.

*

A car prowled across the Bridge
and halted, then turned in a slow curve
under the lamp back over the Canal
with another following on its track,
the rear lights pulsing rose.

A pair of shades. One, in a short skirt,
stirred herself; the other, in black leatherette,
waited back against the railings,
the tip of her cigarette red. Her eyes
and her oyster mouth wet to my thoughts.

My hands framed your throat in
the night air.

Thom Gunn

(1929–2004)

My Sad Captains

Touch

The Hug

Thomson William Gunn was born in Gravesend, Kent, son of a Fleet Street journalist. He went to school in London, living in Hampstead in a home full of books. 'I was mad about Keats and Marlowe when I was fourteen', he says. His parents divorced when he was ten, and his mother (with whom he lived) died at her own hand when he was 15. In his late teens he started reading Auden, who 'seemed so available'. After two years' National Service in the army, he went up to Cambridge. He had read Eliot and just after National Service read Baudelaire, whose impact was decisive. At university he discovered Yeats.

He fell in love, by his own account, at Cambridge, with an American student. To stay with him he applied for American scholarships. In 1954 he went to Stanford on a writing fellowship and he remained in California for the rest of his life, settling in San Francisco in 1961. *Fighting Terms*, his first book, was published: it was the period of the 'angry young men', and Gunn was the first poet among them. At Stanford he began experimenting with syllabics in order to ease himself away from metrical verse. His syllabic poems appeared in *The Sense of Movement* (1957) and *My Sad Captains* (1961). *In Touch* (1967) he achieved a serviceable free verse. Possessing new formal resources, he kept faith with the old, too: certain kinds of statement (elegiac, celebratory, reflective) required metre and stanza, but poems which did not wish to stand back from experience, poems of process, required free verse. In the LSD poems in *Moly* (1971), the dark unsettling poems of *Jack Straw's Castle* (1976), the AIDs elegies in *Man with Night Sweats* (1992) quite as much as in the early verse, one pleasure is to witness the poet overcoming formal challenges.

Gunn discovered Marianne Moore, William Carlos Williams, Pound and Lawrence. The early poems deal with the themes of free will and individual responsibility ('Sartrean Existentialism'), which one critic described as a 'voluntary commitment to the irrational' in a world without intrinsic meanings. Early in Gunn's career Larkin's emotional economy was contrasted with Gunn's emotional profligacy: heroisms were not out of place for Gunn, despite the scaled-down age – heroic or excessive action, expression through the body, its beauty and the risks it takes. The early poems express isolation: the watcher, the watched, the historically singled out, and the survivor. Posing, acting and enacting; they possess a sense of role play, assuming an attitude if not a voice – these are things the subjects of the poems do. Gunn either celebrates wholeness and self-sufficiency, or he laments separation. Isolation becomes increasingly a burden. The poems move, through drug experiences, through love, comradeship and community, beyond the singular self. The occasions of his poetry become more diverse and, in his last book, more sombre. 'I have invented roots', he said.

He was one of the great teachers of British poets, his instruction being by example. He understood, as few before him had, the relation of language to form and of form to occasion, the appropriateness, as it were, the proper decorum, and he showed how such terms as 'decorum' were not precious but part of the necessary toolkit of the poet. Gunn is a late Romantic with a keen classical eye for issues of art, and he left the language of poetry and the discipline of criticism the richer by his examples.

My Sad Captains

One by one they appear in
the darkness: a few friends, and
a few with historical
names. How late they start to shine!
but before they fade they stand
perfectly embodied, all

the past lapping them like a
cloak of chaos. They were men
who, I thought, lived only to
renew the wasteful force they
spent with each hot convulsion.
They remind me, distant now.

True, they are not at rest yet,
but now they are indeed
apart, winnowed from failures,
they withdraw to an orbit
and turn with disinterested
hard energy, like the stars.

Touch

You are already
asleep. I lower
myself in next to
you, my skin slightly
numb with the restraint
of habits, the patina of
self, the black frost
of outsideness, so that even
unclothed, it is
a resilient chilly
hardness, a superficially
malleable, dead
rubbery texture.

You are a mound
of bedclothes, where the cat
in sleep braces
its paws against your
calf through the blankets,
and kneads each paw in turn.

Meanwhile and slowly
I feel a is it
my own warmth surfacing or
the ferment of your whole
body that in darkness beneath
the cover is stealing
bit by bit to break
down that chill.
                        You turn and
hold me tightly, do
you know who
I am or am I
your mother or
the nearest human being to
hold on to in a
dreamed pogrom.

What I, now loosened,
sink into is an old
big place, it is

there already, for
you are already
there, and the cat
got there before you, yet
it is hard to locate.
What is more, the place is
not found but seeps
from our touch in
continuous creation, dark
enclosing cocoon round
ourselves alone, dark
wide realm where we
walk with everyone.

You are a mound
of bedclothes,
where the cat
in sleep braces
its paws against your
calf through the
blankets,
and kneads each
paw in turn.

The Hug

It was your birthday, we had drunk and dined
    Half of the night with our old friend
        Who'd showed us in the end
    To a bed I reached in one drunk stride.
        Already I lay snug,
And drowsy with the wine dozed on one side.

I dozed, I slept. My sleep broke on a hug,
    Suddenly, from behind,
In which the full lengths of our bodies pressed:
    Your instep to my heel,
    My shoulder-blades against your chest.
    It was not sex, but I could feel
    The whole strength of your body set,
        Or braced, to mine,
        And locking me to you
    As if we were still twenty-two
    When our grand passion had not yet
        Become familial.
    My quick sleep had deleted all
    Of intervening time and place.
        I only knew
The stay of your secure firm dry embrace.

I dozed, I
slept. My
sleep broke
on a hug

Adrienne
Rich (b. 1929)

The Burning of Paper instead of
Children

Adrienne Rich has become more, not less, radical as she has grown older. She speaks in her essays of the 1970s of re-visioning, a function her poetry sets out to perform. How did she come to terms with feminism and with her own sexuality? For her the process is long and difficult: 'the awakening of consciousness is not like the crossing of a frontier', not like religious conversion – no divine grace descends. It is a becoming conscious – a deliberate, rigorous reconstruction of self.

Adrienne Cecile Rich was born in Baltimore, Maryland. Her father was a pathologist at Johns Hopkins University and a Jew, her mother a southern gentile. In 1951 she graduated from Radcliffe College (Harvard). In the period after her graduation she published two books of poems, enjoyed a Guggenheim Fellowship, married and had three sons. Her first book, *A Change of World* (1951) was selected by Auden for the Yale Younger Poets series.

In the 1960s there was Black Power, the rise of Feminism and the Gay movements. There was the dreadful unwinding of Vietnam. It is necessary to set Rich in these contexts: they provide occasions first for her formal strategies and tentativenesses, then for the emerging assurance that has made her a figure central to the American women's movement and to the liberalization of American poetry.

In retrospect the radical seeds were already sown in the first poems, but it was with *Snapshots of a Daughter-in-Law* (1962) that the important changes began, continuing through her next three collections with their 'political' titles *Necessities of Life* (1966), *Leaflets* (1969), *The Will to Change* (1971). She was teaching Open Admissions at City College, New York, in touch with aspiring writers from every ethnic and social background. The suburban world receded. In that year her father and her husband died. These losses and other experiences led to her controversial volume *Diving into the Wreck* (1973), where she combines her voices – mother, lesbian, teacher, wife and woman. In 'At a Bach Concert' she wrote: 'A too-compassionate art is only half an art. / Only such proud restraining purity / Restores the else-betrayed, too-human heart.' To make a whole art, it was necessary first to fill in the other half, which might mean, for a time, that compassion will give way to a harsh truth-telling, telling the truth not only to the world but to the self. To tell the truth in poetry there have to be forms, words and a will to use them.

To speak clearly of the things she wishes to speak of she needs a *singular* style, not eccentric or idiosyncratic but one which, when it needs to do so, can incorporate prose, the speaking voices of others, a poetry which is open and belongs (she dates her poems scrupulously) to a time in her life and in history – an occasion. The truth always has a context – it is always particular. The words bomb, woman, peace, love, gay, mean one thing in 1951, but something different in 2006 – different not only for the poet who uses them but for the society in which the language lives.

Changes in her poetry from 1951 to 2006 are large. Feminism, lesbianism, political affection and disaffection spoiled her 'good manners'. So too did a sense of the internal alterations of poetry necessary if she was to find, and then tell, the 'truth' of experience as a woman – not confessional strategies that would individuate her, but comradely strategies serviceable as processes for her readers, enabling them to enact for themselves the adjustments her poems proposed.

The Burning of Paper instead of Children

> I was in danger of verbalizing my
> moral impulses out of existence.
>
> *Daniel Berrigan, on trial in Baltimore*

1. My neighbor, a scientist and art-collector, telephones me in a state of violent emotion. He tells me that my son and his, aged eleven and twelve, have on the last day of school burned a mathematics textbook in the backyard. He has forbidden my son to come to his house for a week, and has forbidden his own son to leave the house during that time. "The burning of a book," he says, "arouses terrible sensations in me, memories of Hitler; there are few things that upset me so much as the idea of burning a book."

Back there: the library, walled
with green Britannicas
Looking again
in Dürer's *Complete Works*
for MELANCOLIA, the baffled woman

the crocodiles in Herodotus
the Book of the Dead
the *Trial of Jeanne d'Arc* so blue
I think, It is her color

and they take the book away
because I dream of her too often

love and fear in a house
knowledge of the oppressor
I know it hurts to burn

2. To imagine a time of silence
or few words
a time of chemistry and music

the hollows above your buttocks
traced by my hand
or, *hair is like flesh*, you said

an age of long silence

relief

from this tongue   this slab of limestone
or reinforced concrete
fanatics and traders
dumped on this coast wildgreen clayred
that breathed once
in signals of smoke
sweep of the wind

knowledge of the oppressor
this is the oppressor's language

yet I need it to talk to you

3. *People suffer highly in poverty and it takes dignity and intelligence to overcome this suffering. Some of the suffering are: a child did not had dinner last night: a child steal because he did not have money to buy it: to hear a mother say she do not have money to buy food for her children and to see a child without cloth it will make tears in your eyes.*

(the fracture of order
the repair of speech
to overcome this suffering)

4. We lie under the sheet
after making love, speaking
of loneliness
relieved in a book
relived in a book
so on that page
the clot and fissure
of it appears
words of a man
in pain
a naked word
entering the clot
a hand grasping
through bars:

deliverance

What happens between us
has happened for centuries
we know it from literature

still it happens

sexual jealousy
outflung hand
beating bed

dryness of mouth
after panting

there are books that describe all this
and they are useless

You walk into the woods behind a house
there in that country
you find a temple
built eighteen hundred years ago
you enter without knowing
what it is you enter

so it is with us

no one knows what may happen
though the books tell everything

burn the texts   said Artaud

5. I am composing on the typewriter late at night, thinking of today. How well we all spoke. A language is a map of our failures. Frederick Douglass wrote an English purer than Milton's. People suffer highly in poverty. There are methods but we do not use them. Joan, who could not read, spoke some peasant form of French. Some of the suffering are: it is hard to tell the truth; this is America; I cannot touch you now. In America we have only the present tense. I am in danger. You are in danger. The burning of a book arouses no sensation in me. I know it hurts to burn. There are flames of napalm in Catonsville, Maryland. I know it hurts to burn. The typewriter is overheated, my mouth is burning. I cannot touch you and this is the oppressor's language.

Kamau
Brathwaite
(b. 1930)

Calypso

Kamau Brathwaite was born in Barbados into a middle-class family. He was educated there and at Pembroke College, Cambridge, where he read history. From 1955 to 1962 he taught in Ghana and started a children's theatre there. It was a difficult time for him, but later he revised his view of it, referring to it as a time of growing solidarity and self-discovery. His doctoral thesis at the University of Sussex was on the Jamaican Slave Trade and Creole Society in the Eighteenth Century. He returned to the West Indies and taught history at the University of the West Indies until his retirement.

He has published plays and several major collections of poetry, beginning with *Rights of Passage* (1967), then *Masks* (1968) and *Islands* (1969), which together constituted his first trilogy, *The Arrivants: a new world trilogy* (1973). This was followed by *Other Exiles* (1975), *Mother Poem* (1977), *Sun Poem* (1982), *Third World Poems* (1983), *X/Self* (1987) and *Middle Passages* (1992). Since that time a number of collections, some experimenting with typography and layout, all in one way or another contributing to the ongoing argument of his poems, have appeared.

For Brathwaite English is a colonial, an 'owned' language. He rebels in various ways against it and the values it still seems to him to contain, the distortions of black experience it still seems to impose; and he rebels against his own early poetry and poetic strategies, resembling in this the American poet Leroi Jones (Amiri Baraka), whose later work involves the unweaving of his powerful early poems and their replacement by quite a different kind of power, fuelled less by compassion than by anger.

Brathwaite perceived in prosody what he took to be a crucial tyranny, and his analysis is vehement and subtle, though some see it as reductive and disenabling. The tyranny inheres in the iambic pentameter, which is hostile to native Caribbean speech rhythms (which contain more 'stress'), and in English poetic diction which does not admit Caribbean reality, syntax or diction. For centuries an English curriculum has been imposed in which Caribbean students are made to read poems about snow and daffodils rather than their own weather, their own plants and creatures. The English tradition is less a resource, he believes, than a form of impoverishment and constraint. Brathwaite tries to create a new poetry based on Jamaican speech patterns, unmetred, aurally emphatic and, on the page, more and more visually articulated.

Like Derek Walcott's, his 'landscape' is a seascape of islands and oceans in various states of weather. His Shakespeare is *The Tempest* and Caliban becomes his protagonist. 'Ah brave third world!' Walcott exclaims, being devoted to the same play for other reasons. Brathwaite tries to provide his culture with an epic. His trilogies are Homeric in scope and aspiration and have a vigour and flow, a specifically oral quality, that achieves at times, momentarily, an Homeric timbre, though he cannot resist didacticism for long. While Walcott tries to create an accessible high culture, Brathwaite tries for a culture grown from and for the 'grass roots' which he identifies, defines and speaks for.

Calypso

from Islands and Exiles

1

The stone had skidded arc'd and bloomed into islands:
Cuba and San Domingo
Jamaica and Puerto Rico
Grenada Guadeloupe Bonaire

curved stone hissed into reef
wave teeth fanged into clay
white splash flashed into spray
Bathsheba Montego Bay

bloom of the arcing summers...

2

The islands roared into green plantations
ruled by silver sugar cane
sweat and profit
cutlass profit
islands ruled by sugar cane

And of course it was a wonderful time
a profitable hospitable well-worth-your-time
when captains carried receipts for rices
letters spices wigs
opera glasses swaggering asses
debtors vices pigs

O it was a wonderful time
an elegant benevolent redolent time –
and young Mrs. P.'s quick irrelevant crime
at four o'clock in the morning...

3

But what of black Sam
with the big splayed toes
and the shoe black shiny skin?

He carries bucketfuls of water
'cause his Ma's just had another daughter.

And what of John with the European name
who went to school and dreamt of fame
his boss one day called him a fool
and the boss hadn't even been to school...

sweat and profit
cutlass profit
islands ruled by
sugar cane

4

Steel drum steel drum
hit the hot calypso dancing
hot rum hot rum
who goin' stop this bacchanalling?

For we glance the banjo
dance the limbo
grow our crops by maljo

have loose morals
gather corals
father out neighbour's quarrels

perhaps when they come
with their cameras and straw
hats: sacred pink tourists from the frozen Nawth

we should get down to those
white beaches
where if we don't wear breeches

it becomes an island dance
Some people doin' well
while others are catchin' hell

o the boss gave our Johnny the sack
though we beg him please
please to take 'im back

so the boy now nigratin' overseas...

Steel drum steel drum
hit the hot calypso dancing
hot rum hot rum
who goin' stop this bacchanalling?

Ted Hughes

(1930–1998)

Wodwo

From *Two Legends*

*God Help the Wolf after Whom the Dogs
Do Not Bark*

Ted Hughes was born in Mytholmroyd, Yorkshire. The landscape of his poems is here, actual settings in a place sparsely inhabited, where nature is near at hand. It is an austere, craggy and – apart from the vales – a treeless area with big skies and the ruins of industry: mills and pits. When he was seven his family moved to Mexborough, where he went to school. The natural world and his father's experience as a First World War veteran were determining themes. At 15 he was writing verse.

Before he went up to Cambridge he did his National Service as an RAF ground wireless mechanic in East Yorkshire, where he spent his time reading Shakespeare. At Cambridge he changed from English to anthropology and archaeology. In 1954 he graduated and married the American poet Sylvia Plath. Hughes's first book, *Hawk in the Rain*, appeared in 1957.

Is Hughes a 'nature poet' or are his animals and images of nature in fact symbolic enactments of human types and aggressions? *Lupercal* (1960), his second substantial collection, raises the question insistently. His single-minded creatures and his relishing in them of violence and survival, give off – if read politically – a treacherous note. The Hawk, Thrush, Pike and Bull are not only physical but moral centres of their worlds; the poet, by withholding comment, seems to assent to their natures.

For five years his relationship with Sylvia Plath was creatively fruitful. They separated in 1962 and the formal and imaginative frame of his poetry altered. Each substantial collection that followed approached the world of the early poems from a different angle, the poet moving from the literal-seeming into the allegorical and mythological. *Wodwo* (1967), and his most celebrated and controversial book, the sequence *Crow* (1970), paint him into a thematic corner from which he escaped only much later. *Birthday Letters* (1998), evoking his relationship with Plath, living and dead, attempts a new prosody and an understated narrative out of character with what has come before.

When Hughes's world and the natural or animal world coincide, the best poems occur, or when Hughes – recognizing this tendency in his work – invents an animal, 'Wodwo' for instance, borrowed from *Gawain and the Green Knight* to do within the natural world what Hughes is doing through it, defining a nature – an identity. D.H. Lawrence subjects us to violence and pain, 'opens' us, in order to be filled and fulfilled. Hughes at times seems to want to open us to be hurt. In *Wodwo* literal creatures give way to imaginary ones, nightmare is all about us, and in *Crow* a metaphysical, historical and individual nightmare, cast in anthropological terms, occurs. In *Tales from Ovid* he steps into quite another world, a classical world not made of marble, not ruined, but a place in which extreme action is not the only option, where the lyrical has its place and psychology is more nuanced and various than it has been before. He is not translating Ovid but adapting him, or working in fruitful collaboration. He has set himself free, by an act of will, of the repetitive and narrowing world of his earlier writing. His form of candour was exorcism, working emotions and impulses out through images and complex verbal structures. The freedom of *Tales from Ovid* does not reject but incorporates in a larger pattern what has gone before. In *Birthday Letters* he takes a further step, addressing a loss without self-pity and with as much precision as his memory will allow, answering with unusual quietness and with his eyes averted from those decades of savage and malicious critics and gossips. He is trying to resolve a relationship which was his and hers but has become legendary – emblematic.

Wodwo

What am I? Nosing here, turning leaves over
Following a faint stain on the air to the river's edge
I enter water. What am I to split
The glassy grain of water looking upward I see the bed
Of the river above me upside down very clear
What am I doing here in mid-air? Why do I find
this frog so interesting as I inspect its most secret
interior and make it my own? Do these weeds
know me and name me to each other have they
seen me before, do I fit in their world? I seem
separate from the ground and not rooted but dropped
out of nothing casually I've no threads
fastening me to anything I can go anywhere
I seem to have been given the freedom
of this place what am I then? And picking
bits of bark off this rotten stump gives me
no pleasure and it's no use so why do I do it
me and doing that have coincided very queerly
But what shall I be called am I the first
have I an owner what shape am I what
shape am I am I huge if I go
to the end on this way past these trees and past these trees
till I get tired that's touching one wall of me
for the moment if I sit still how everything
stops to watch me I suppose I am the exact centre
but there's all this what is it roots
roots roots roots and here's the water
again very queer but I'll go on looking

From Two Legends

II
Black is the wet otter's head, lifted.
Black is the rock, plunging in foam.
Black is the gall lying on the bed of the blood.

Black is the earth-globe, one inch under,
An egg of blackness
Where the sun and moon alternate their weathers

To hatch a crow, a black rainbow
Bent in emptiness
                                        over emptiness
But flying

God Help the Wolf after Whom the Dogs Do Not Bark

There you met it–the mystery of hatred.
After your billions of years in anonymous matter
That was where you were found – and promptly hated.
You tried your utmost to reach and touch those people
With gifts of yourself –
Just like your first words as a toddler
When you rushed at every visitor to the house
Clasping their legs and crying: 'I love you! I love you!'
Just as you had danced for your father
In the home of anger – gifts of your life
To sweeten his slow death and mix yourself in it
Where he lay propped on the couch,
To sugar the bitterness of his raging death.

You searched for yourself to go on giving it
As if after the nightfall of his going
You danced on in the dark house,
Eight years old, in your tinsel.

Searching for yourself, in the dark, as you danced,
Floundering a little, crying softly,
Like somebody searching for somebody drowning
In dark water,
Listening for them – in panic at losing
Those listening seconds from your searching –
Then dancing wilder in the silence.

The Colleges lifted their heads. It did seem
You disturbed something just perfected
That they were holding carefully, all of a piece,
Till the glue dried. And as if
Reporting some felony to the police
They let you know that you were not John Donne.
You no longer care. Did you save their names?
But then they let you know, day by day,
Their contempt for everything you attempted,
Took pains to inject their bile, as for your health,
Into your morning coffee. Even signed
Their homeopathic letters,
Envelopes full of carefully broken glass
To lodge behind your eyes so you would see

Nobody wanted your dance,
Nobody wanted your strange glitter – your floundering
Drowning life and your effort to save yourself,
Treading water, dancing the dark turmoil,
Looking for something to give –
                                Whatever you found
They bombarded with splinters,
Derision, mud – the mystery of that hatred.

Searching for yourself, in the dark, as you danced

Derek
Walcott
(b. 1930)

Adios, Carenage

Apoet, says Seamus Heaney, must also 'go beyond himself and take on the otherness of the world in works that remain his own yet offer rights-of-way to everybody else'. Derek Walcott has 'found a language woven out of dialect and literature, neither folksy nor condescending, a singular idiom evolved out of one man's inherited divisions and obsessions, an idiom which allows an older life to exult in itself and yet at the same time keeps the cool of "the new".'

Walcott was born in Castries, St Lucia. His father, a civil servant, died when he was one. His mother was a schoolteacher. Both the poet's grandfathers were white Europeans, both his grandmothers were of African origin. With his brother he published his first two books, *25 Poems* (1948) and *Epitaph for the Young: XII Cantos* (1949). He attended the University of the West Indies in Kingston, Jamaica, graduating in 1953. In 1959 he helped to found the Trinidad Theatre Workshop, which he directed until 1977. Then he went to the United States to teach.

His 'real books' of poems began to appear later: *In a Green Night: Poems 1948-1960* (London, 1962) and *Selected Poems* (New York, 1964). Robert Graves declared, 'Derek Walcott handles English with a closer understanding of its inner magic than most (if not any) of his contemporaries.' Then followed *The Castaway and Other Poems* (1965), *The Gulf and Other Poems* (1969), *Another Life* (1973), *Sea Grapes* (1976), *The Star-Apple Kingdom* (1979), *The Fortunate Traveller* (1981), *Midsummer* (1984), *Collected Poems 1948–1984* (1986), *The Arkansas Testament* (1987) and the epic *Omeros* (1993).

Half of Walcott's ancestors were forced to come to the new world. He now masters elements of European culture, such as language and genre, and reforms them so that the epic of ancient heroes can be used to draw into heroic lineaments the experiences of fishermen and small traders.

Our literary sense of the West Indies was shaped by V.S. Naipaul, the *Biswas* vision (1961). He is called 'Old Misery' by some in the Caribbean. *The Middle Passage* (1962) speaks of the people of Coronie in Surinam: 'The history of the islands can never be satisfactorily told. Brutality is not the only difficulty. History is built around achievement and creation; and nothing was created in the West Indies.' Derek Walcott writes in 1973, in response: 'Nothing will always be created in the West Indies for quite a long time, because whatever will come out of there is like nothing one has ever seen before.' In 1979 Walcott's 'The Schooner *Flight*' in *The Star-Apple Kingdom* proposes a new West Indian identity. It is a key work in the emergence of Caribbean English poetry.

Walcott remembers an earlier time. In 'Sainte Lucie' (1976) he says 'Come back to me my language' – the language of youth and innocence; also of 'tribe' and 'community'. But he had begun to change his language. In *The Arkansas Testament* he writes largely in standard English, highlighting how the French words and the native words for different things and creatures give them a different force and identity. So – when he brings Homeric themes and techniques into the American Mediterranean and the thousands of islands of the Caribbean – Homer is altered, and all that Homer has meant to English literature is subtly altered, by the new content, the new politics which do not replicate but extend the old. It is a matter of making connections in terms that distort neither the classical nor the neo-classical culture. Walcott's resistance to political imperatives and ideologies is itself heroic.

Adios, Carenage

From *The Schooner 'Flight'*

In idle August, while the sea soft,
and leaves of brown islands stick to the rim
of this Caribbean, I blow out the light
by the dreamless face of Maria Concepcion
to ship as a seaman on the schooner *Flight*.
Out in the yard turning gray in the dawn,
I stood like a stone and nothing else move
but the cold sea rippling like galvanize
and the nail holes of stars in the sky roof,
till a wind start to interfere with the trees.
I pass me dry neighbor sweeping she yard
as I went downhill, and I nearly said:
'Sweep soft, you witch, 'cause she don't sleep hard,'
but the bitch look through me like I was dead.
A route taxi pull up, park-lights still on.
The driver size up my bags with a grin:
'This time, Shabine, like you really gone!'
I ain't answer the ass, I simply pile in
the back seat and watch the sky burn
above Laventille pink as the gown
in which the woman I left was sleeping,
and I look in the rearview and see a man
exactly like me, and the man was weeping
for the houses, the street, that whole fucking island.

Christ have mercy on all sleeping things!
From that dog rotting down Wrightson Road
to when I was a dog on these streets;
if loving these islands must be my load,
out of corruption my soul takes wings,
But they had started to poison my soul
with their big house, big car, big-time bohbohl,
coolie, nigger, Syrian, and French Creole,
so I leave it for them and their carnival —
I taking a sea-bath, I gone down the road.
I know these islands from Monos to Nassau,
a rusty head sailor with sea-green eyes
that they nickname Shabine, the patois for
any red nigger, and I, Shabine, saw
when these slums of empire was paradise.

if loving these
islands must
be my load,
out of
corruption my
soul takes
wings

I'm just a red nigger who love the sea,
I had a sound colonial education,
I have Dutch, nigger, and English in me,
and either I'm nobody, or I'm a nation,

But Maria Concepcion was all my thought
watching the sea heaving up and down
as the port side of dories, schooners, and yachts
was painted afresh by the strokes of the sun
signing her name with every reflection;
I knew when dark-haired evening put on
her bright silk at sunset, and, folding the sea,
sidled under the sheet with her starry laugh,
that there'd be no rest, there'd be no forgetting.
Is like telling mourners round the graveside
about resurrection, they want the dead back,
so I smile to myself as the bow rope untied
and the *Flight* swing seaward: 'Is no use repeating
that the sea have more fish. I ain't want her
dressed in the sexless light of a seraph,
I want those round brown eyes like a marmoset, and
till the day when I can lean back and laugh,
those claws that tickled my back on sweating
Sunday afternoons, like a crab on wet sand.'
As I worked, watching the rotting waves come
past the bow that scissor the sea like silk,
I swear to you all, by my mother's milk,
by the stars that shall fly from tonight's furnace,
that I loved them, my children, my wife, my home;
I loved them as poets love the poetry
that kills them, as drowned sailors the sea.

You ever look up from some lonely beach
and see a far schooner? Well, when I write
this poem, each phrase go be soaked in salt;
I go draw and knot every line as tight
as ropes in this rigging; in simple speech
my common language go be the wind,
my pages the sails of the schooner *Flight*.
But let me tell you how this business begin. […]

I loved them as poets love the poetry that kills them, as drowned sailors the sea.

Geoffrey Hill

(b. 1932)

Genesis

September Song

Ovid in the Third Reich

In his public readings, Geoffrey Hill speaks his poems clearly, attending to syntax, diction, pace and pause, without dramatizing. He hardly looks up at his audience at all. A poem is complete in itself and requires of the reader only fidelity. *Only* fidelity? This is the hardest thing for the reading voice to do, to withhold subjectivity, to efface all but receptive intelligence and the sound of voice, in the poem's service. A poem should contain all that is required for its understanding. The discipline the poems require of the reader they require all the more intensely of the poet. A poem is not a meditation but a making that must be true to the experience it creates, often across languages and across time: the poem has to know the world from which the voice is speaking so that the voice can speak. Hill was born in Bromsgrove, Worcestershire. It is the landscape of the Malverns, of the opening of *Piers Ploughman*, of Edward Elgar and Ivor Gurney and Housman. Woven into *Mercian Hymns* is as much as we need to know about his childhood: the intelligent child humoured if not understood by his family (his father was in the police), studying and writing alone into the night. He went from grammar school to Keble College, Oxford. There he wrote his first major poem, 'Genesis', at the age of 20.

He taught at Leeds where he became Professor, then at Emmanuel College, Cambridge as a Fellow, then to Boston University in 1988. *For the Unfallen* (1959) was his first book; it has been followed at irregular intervals by *King Log* (1968), *Mercian Hymns* (1971), *Tenebrae* (1978), *The Mystery of the Charity of Charles Peguy* (1983), *The Lords of Limit: Essays on Literature and Ideas* (1984), *Collected Poems* (1985) and a flurry of new collections since *Canaan* (1996). He translated Ibsen's *Brand* for the National Theatre.

The poet's occasions are unusual. When he, or the subject he is writing for, cannot feel or cannot act (feeling is a form of action) the poem happens: in the wake of battle, of torture, or of unfulfilment in love. The compulsion, the pressure behind the poem, is *frustrated* sense, a need to articulate, combined with an intense reticence which limits the area in which he will allow the language to work. He is drawn to the Modernists – Eliot in particular is crucial to his formation – and it is not only the Eliot of *The Waste Land* but the later Anglican Eliot that he unfashionably learns from. He does not write dramatic monologues but soliloquies. His voices speak from within their experience, not about it. There is imbalance, the poems suggest, in all relations: in love, family, politics and religion. Elegy is Hill's dominant mode, but not mellifluous elegy: he is often harshly consonantal, a poet of phrases rather than cadences. Yet the language and terms of liturgy and of church and secular music recur not only in titles – Hymns, Canticles, Song-Book, Requiem, 'Funeral Music', Fantasia – but in the structuring of the poems.

Latterly he has described himself as an Anglican, as if the long discipline of the poems has made belief tenable. His is an Anglican England. His vision of his country Donald Davie described as patriotic, and no weaker word will do. He understands the great divisions, not least that between the North and South and Robin Hood versus King Arthur. His own landscape is the Midlands which has always been – even in the time of the medieval poet John Gower – the mediating landscape, where a poet can talk in both directions, negotiating between the hierarchical South and the democratic-anarchic North.

Genesis

I

Against the burly air I strode
Crying the miracles of God.

And first I brought the sea to bear
Upon the dead weight of the land;
And the waves flourished at my prayer,
The rivers spawned their sand.

And where the streams were salt and full
The tough pig-headed salmon strove,
Ramming the ebb, in the tide's pull,
To reach the steady hills above.

II

The second day I stood and saw
The osprey plunge with triggered claw,
Feathering blood along the shore,
To lay the living sinew bare.

And the third day I cried: 'Beware
The soft-voiced owl, the ferret's smile,
The hawk's deliberate stoop in air,
Cold eyes, and bodies hooped in steel,
Forever bent upon the kill.'

III

And I renounced, on the fourth day,
This fierce and unregenerate clay,

Building as a huge myth for man
The watery Leviathan,

And made the long-winged albatross
Scour the ashes of the sea
Where Capricorn and Zero cross,
A brooding immortality –
Such as the charmèd phoenix has
In the unwithering tree.

IV

The phoenix burns as cold as frost;
And, like a legendary ghost,
The phantom-bird goes wild and lost,
Upon a pointless ocean tossed.

So, the fifth day, I turned again
To flesh and blood and the blood's pain.

V

On the sixth day, as I rode
In haste about the works of God,
With spurs I plucked the horse's blood.

By blood we live, the hot, the cold,
To ravage and redeem the world:
There is no bloodless myth will hold.

And by Christ's blood are men made free
Though in close shrouds their bodies lie
Under the rough pelt of the sea;

Though earth has rolled beneath her weight
The bones that cannot bear the light.

By blood we live,
the hot, the cold,
To ravage and
redeem the world:
There is no
bloodless myth
will hold.

September Song

born 19.6.32 – deported 24.9.42

Undesirable you may have been, untouchable
you were not. Not forgotten
or passed over at the proper time.

As estimated, you died. Things marched,
sufficient, to that end.
Just so much Zyklon and leather, patented
terror, so many routine cries.

 (I have made
an elegy for myself it
is true)

September fattens on vines. Roses
flake from the wall. The smoke
of harmless fires drifts to my eyes.

This is plenty. This is more than enough.

The smoke
of harmless
fires drifts to
my eyes.

Ovid in the Third Reich

non peccat, quaecumque potest pecasse negare,
solaque famosam culpa professa facit.
                    Ovid, Amores, III, xiv

I love my work and my children. God
Is distant, difficult. Things happen.
Too near the ancient troughs of blood
Innocence is no earthly weapon.

I have learned one thing: not to look down
So much upon the damned. They, in their sphere,
Harmonise strangely with the divine
Love. I, in mine, celebrate the love-choir.

Innocence is no
earthly weapon.

Sylvia **Plath**

(1932–1963)

I n Sylvia Plath's poems 'The fountains are dry and the roses over.' Fountains, not rivers and lakes; roses, not thistles and brambles. She is the deliberate poet; she devises strategies; she competes for space and attention. She is experimental, setting herself exercises. She is an ironist. 'I think my poems come immediately out of the sensuous and emotional experiences I have,' she said, 'but I must say I cannot sympathize with these cries from the heart that are informed by nothing except a needle or a knife or whatever it is.' She added: 'I believe that one should be able to control and manipulate experiences, even the most terrifying – like madness, being tortured, this kind of experience – and one should be able to manipulate these experiences with an informed and intelligent mind. I think that personal experience shouldn't be a kind of shut box and mirror-looking narcissistic experience. I believe it should be generally relevant, to such things as Hiroshima and Dachau, and so on.'

'And so on' reveals how much of an artist she is – how devastating experiences of the century become a resource. Anger, anxiety, fear and love – these primary emotions can dispose of the hard facts of existence as they wish. A poetry of extremity must first be poetry. And where Plath is concerned, getting at the poetry is complicated by the problem of biography: her relationship with her mother and father; her displacement as an American in England; her marriage to an unusual Englishman, Ted Hughes; the creation of a family; the end of their relationship, her suicide. The poems are read as oblique autobiography yet no biographer has access to the human content of events.

She was born in Boston. Her first poem was published when she was eight years old, in the *Boston Sunday Herald*. Her father, of German extraction, was an entomologist, a professor at Boston University. He died when she was eight, the first of several traumatic desertions. Her mother filled the space he left with a directive love which the young poet relished and resented. *Letters Home* tells the story of their complex relationship. She graduated from Smith College (after a severe nervous breakdown induced by overwork) in 1955, and attended Lowell's poetry course at Harvard. Anne Sexton became a close friend, writing in the aftermath of her mental breakdown, and some of Plath's poems draw with surprising freedom on Sexton, borrowing lines, cadences and strategies. Sexton's first book, *To Bedlam and Part Way Back*, appeared in the same year as Plath's *The Colossus* (1960), and became raw material (with other, rawer material) for Plath's major poems in *Ariel*, published two years after her death. Sexton revealed to Plath the force of simple rhyme and rhythm, the magic of nursery rhyme darkened by time, of fairy tale where a happy ending somehow doesn't happen.

After Smith College, Plath was awarded a Fulbright scholarship and travelled to Cambridge, in England, where she met Ted Hughes and they married in 1956. She died in 1963, the year in which her autobiographical novel *The Bell Jar* was published. In 1981 Ted Hughes assembled the *Collected Poems*.

In the two or three months after her marriage was over, late in 1962, Plath wrote the bulk of the celebrated poems in *Ariel* at great speed and with astonishing assurance. She thought she knew how extraordinary they were, but there was nobody to reassure her. She was hungry for response, for affectionate recognition, but her human intensities and transparent unhappiness kept those who might have responded to her that terribly cold winter at bay.

Daddy

You do not do, you do not do
Any more, black shoe
In which I have lived like a foot
For thirty years, poor and white,
Barely daring to breathe or Achoo.

Daddy, I have had to kill you.
You died before I had time –
Marble-heavy, a bag full of God,
Ghastly statue with one grey toe
Big as a Frisco seal

And a head in the freakish Atlantic
Where it pours bean green over blue
In the waters off beautiful Nauset.
I used to pray to recover you.
Ach, du.

In the German tongue, in the Polish town
Scraped flat by the roller
Of wars, wars, wars.
But the name of the town is common.
My Polack friend

Says there are a dozen or two.
So I never could tell where you
Put your foot, your root,
I never could talk to you.
The tongue stuck in my jaw.

It stuck in a barbed wire snare.
Ich, ich, ich, ich,
I could hardly speak.
I thought every German was you.
And the language obscene

An engine, an engine,
Chuffing me off like a Jew.
A Jew to Dachau, Auschwitz, Belsen.
I began to talk like a Jew.
I think I may well be a Jew.

The snows of the Tyrol, the clear beer of Vienna
Are not very pure or true.
With my gypsy ancestress and my weird luck
And my Taroc pack and my Taroc pack
I may be a bit of a Jew.

The snows of
the Tyrol, the
clear beer of
Vienna
Are not very
pure or true.

I have always been scared of *you*,
With your Luftwaffe, your gobbledygoo.
And your neat moustache
And your Aryan eye, bright blue.
Panzer-man, panzer-man, O You –

Not God but a swastika
So black no sky could squeak through.
Every woman adores a Fascist,
The boot in the face, the brute
Brute heart of a brute like you.

You stand at the blackboard, daddy,
In the picture I have of you,
A cleft in your chin instead of your foot
But no less a devil for that, no not
Any less the black man who

Bit my pretty red heart in two.
I was ten when they buried you.
At twenty I tried to die
And get back, back, back to you.
I thought even the bones would do.

But they pulled me out of the sack,
And they stuck me together with glue.
And then I knew what to do.
I made a model of you,
A man in black with a Meinkampf look.

And a love of the rack and the screw.
And I said I do, I do.
So daddy, I'm finally through.
The black telephone's off at the root,
The voices just can't worm through.

If I've killed one man, I've killed two –
The vampire who said he was you
And drank my blood for a year,
Seven years, if you want to know.
Daddy, you can lie back now.

There's a stake in your fat black heart
And the villagers never liked you.
They are dancing and stamping on you.
They always *knew* it was you.
Daddy, daddy, you bastard, I'm through.

I have always
been scared
of *you*,
With your
Luftwaffe, your
gobbledygoo.

Les
Murray (b. 1938)

An Absolutely Ordinary Rainbow

Cockspur Bush

The Meaning of Existence

Les Murray is heard as 'the Australian voice', but he is an eccentric one: a rural poet speaking for an urban culture and a Roman Catholic speaking in a largely secular society. He insists that every form of expression is poetry: some people happen do it with language, others with dance, or skating, or chopping timber. Poetry, a universal making, a universal *kind* of engagement, is not, in his view, confined to language, though his own is. In the wake of the long disregard for Australian writing in Britain and America, he is a sharp critic and a warm advocate.

Australia is a coastal culture, a necklace of habitation around a largely 'dead heart'. Its first poet was the son of transported convicts – Charles Harpur, whom Murray celebrates as a nineteenth-century presence embodying the Europe–Australia split, hostile at once to England and to his own society. Murray strikes effectively against 'that imperial trap of exclusion', making the map of the century's poetry larger. He also writes within a tradition described by Scottish writers, Hugh MacDiarmid and Sorley MacLean; by Frost and Jeffers; by a legion of poets he has read attentively and celebrated in essays or in tributes, except for the Modernists. His impatience with Pound, Eliot and the rest is resolute.

He celebrates the environment of his childhood, the farm he was born on and its creatures, which he loved because he felt at home with them when he did not feel comfortable at school. He evokes the poetry of gossip and 'bush balladry'. His father was at the heart of things and his stories are behind many of the poems. It is from this background that Murray learns the intimacy of his address, direct, subtle but always including. 'An Absolutely Ordinary Rainbow' exhibits his main qualities. It tells a story. It is *democratic*, about how people respond, and the urban world is presented sympathetically. It is religious but not doctrinaire, about a man weeping publicly and his effect on others – about the grace of acknowledged grief. It is an emotive poem, designed to be read aloud, but not a performance poem and not written on any audience's terms. Most importantly, its anti-Modernist drift means that Murray's intention is to '*make it present*' rather than 'make it new'.

Murray's collections begin in 1965 with *The Ilex Tree*. His verse novel *The Boys who Stole the Funeral* (1980) is 140 sonnets, a modest precursor to his massive verse novel *Fredy Neptune* (1998), a story that takes its protagonist through the history of the latter half of the twentieth century in a series of adventures and reflections. His first substantial book to be published outside Australia was *The Vernacular Republic: Poems 1961–1981* (1982). It put his poems not only on the map but at the centre of it. Later books include *The Daylight Moon* (1987), *Dog Fox Field* (1990), the large *Collected Poems* (1991), *Translations from the Natural World* (1993) and *Subhuman Redneck Poems* (1996), awarded – ironically in view of his attitude to Modernism – the T.S. Eliot Prize of 1996.

'It would be as myopic to regard Mr Murray as an Australian poet as to call Yeats an Irishman,' Joseph Brodsky said in his over-emphatic generosity. 'He is, quite simply, the one by whom the language lives.' And Derek Walcott: 'There is no poetry in the English language so rooted in its sacredness, so broad-leafed in its pleasures, and yet so intimate and conversational.' Murray is a poet of the sacred, but a sacredness that rises out of this, our material world – the world of our language.

An Absolutely Ordinary Rainbow

The word goes round Repins,
the murmur goes round Lorenzinis,
at Tattersalls, men look up from sheets of numbers,
the Stock Exchange scribblers forget the chalk in their hands
and men with bread in their pockets leave the Greek Club:
There's a fellow crying in Martin Place. They can't stop him.

The traffic in George Street is banked up for half a mile
and drained of motion. The crowds are edgy with talk
and more crowds come hurrying. Many run into the back streets
which minutes ago were busy main streets, pointing:
There's a fellow weeping down there. No one can stop him.

The man we surround, the man no one approaches
simply weeps, and does not cover it, weeps
not like a child, not like the wind, like a man
and does not declaim it, not beat his breast, not even
sob very loudly — yet the dignity of his weeping

holds us back from his space, the hollow he makes about him
in the midday light, in his pentagram of sorrow,
and uniforms back in the crowd who tried to seize him
stare out at him, and feel, with amazement, their minds
longing for tears as children for a rainbow.

Some will say, in the years to come, a halo
or force stood around him. There was no such thing.
Some will say they were shocked and would have stopped him
but they will not have been there. The fiercest manhood,
the toughest reserve, the slickest wit amongst us

trembles with silence, and burns with unexpected
judgements of peace. Some in the concourse scream
who thought themselves happy. Only the smallest children
and such as look out of Paradise come near him
and sit at his feet, with dogs and dusty pigeons.

Ridiculous, says a man near me, and stops
his mouth with his hands, as if it uttered vomit —
and I see a woman, shining, stretch out her hand
and shake as she receives the gift of weeping;
as many as follow her also receive it

And many weep for sheer acceptance, and more
refuse to weep for fear of all acceptance,
but the weeping man, like the earth, requires nothing,

the man who weeps ignores us, and cries out
of his writhen face and ordinary body

not words, but grief, not messages, but sorrow
hard as the earth, sheer, present as the sea —
and when he stops, he simply walks between us
mopping his face with the dignity of one
man who has wept, and now has finished weeping.

Evading believers, he hurries off down Pitt Street.

Cockspur Bush

I am lived. I am died.
I was two-leafed three times, and grazed,
but then I was stemmed and multiplied,
sharp-thorned and caned, nested and raised,
earth-salt by sun-sugar. I was innerly sung
by thrushes who need fear no eyed skin thing.
Finched, ant-run, flowered, I am given the years
in now fewer berries, now more of sling
out over directions of luscious dung.
Of water the crankshaft, of gases the gears
my shape is cattle-pruned to a crown spread sprung
above the starve-gut instinct to make prairies
of everywhere. My thorns are stuck with caries
of mice and rank lizards by the butcher bird.
Inches in, baby seed-screamers get supplied.
I am lived and died in, vine woven, multiplied.

The Meaning of Existence

Everything except language
knows the meaning of existence.
Trees, planets, rivers, time
know nothing else. They express it
moment by moment as the universe.

Even this fool of a body
lives it in part, and would
have full dignity within it
but for the ignorant freedom
of my talking mind.

Everything
except language
knows the
meaning of
existence.

Seamus **Heaney**

(b. 1939)

Punishment

The Guttural Muse

The Haw Lantern

Seamus Heaney was born in Mossbawn, County Derry, Northern Ireland. His father was a Roman Catholic farmer. The eldest of nine children, Heaney won a scholarship to St Columb's College, Derry, where he boarded. 'My sensibility,' he said in an interview, 'was formed by the dolorous murmurings of the rosary, and the generally Marian quality of devotion. The reality that was addressed was maternal, and the posture was one of supplication.' He learned patience, 'the best virtue', and the 'Hail Mary' struck him as a 'better poem' than the 'Our Father', because it is 'faintly amorous'. Already poetry was colouring, or displacing, faith.

He attended Queen's University, Belfast, became a schoolteacher, then returned to his university as a lecturer in 1965. The next year he published his first collection, *Death of a Naturalist*. He taught at Queen's until 1972, and during that time his second and third collections appeared: *Door into the Dark* (1969) and *Wintering Out* (1972). He spent four years in County Wicklow (*North* was published in 1975), then moved to Dublin. *Field Work* appeared in 1979, with his first *Selected Poems*. In 1984 he was appointed Boylston Professor of Rhetoric and Oratory at Harvard and in 1989 Professor of Poetry at Oxford. He has been prolific: *Station Island* and *Sweeney Astray* (1984), *The Haw Lantern* and *New and Selected Poems 1966–1987* (1987), *Seeing Things* (1991) and *The Spirit Level* (1996) and further collections followed, along with anthologies, introductions and three essay collections. In 1995 he was awarded the Nobel Prize for Literature.

For all his travels, he remains a poet with a locality and landscape, though he is displaced from it as he was once displaced in it. His early displacement was due to the fact that he did not have a rural vocation: he expresses through his evocations a warm solidarity with what he left behind, a nostalgia for the past which becomes a nostalgia for the present, which he can watch but cannot in conscience fully engage. This failure of engagement is one of the most powerful themes of his poetry and a testament to its political and social integrity.

He began writing when he began teaching: an urge to compete with R.S. Thomas and with Ted Hughes, both classroom poets. He becomes political when his environment is politicized – when the pull of history becomes too hard to resist. To what extent do external factors promote his reputation ask those who resent his success. The Troubles are not external to one whose community is riven by them, nor do they become external when he leaves. We have to connect where he came from with where he has gone, what he was with what he now is, and the uses made of him and his resistance to or complicity with those uses.

Heaney hears different dialects and accents and they mean different things. 'The Guttural Muse' in *Field Work*, the book he struggled hardest for, brings together two experiences: the image of the slimy doctor fish and the sounds of people talking a 'redemptive' dialect outside the poet's hotel window (sounds which assuaged his sense of isolation and aloneness and let him see 'beyond confusion'). Heaney's model is not Joyce and not the great Irish *Tain*. It is Auden, who teaches that the poet's tasks are making, judging and knowing. He moves from a specific landscape to a wider sense of Ireland – the shape that it is in a map, the roads that intersect it and the histories that divide it. There is a tentativeness in his growth, a willingness to be blown off course and a self-knowledge sufficient to right the rudder and go on, following that sixth sense he speaks of.

Punishment

I can feel the tug
of the halter at the nape
of her neck, the wind
on her naked front.

It blows her nipples
to amber beads,
it shakes the frail rigging
of her ribs.

I can see her drowned
body in the bog,
the weighing stone,
the floating rods and boughs.

Under which at first
she was a barked sapling
that is dug up
oak-bone, brain-firkin:

her shaved head
like a stubble of black corn,
her blindfold a soiled bandage,
her noose a ring

to store
the memories of love.
Little adulteress,
before they punished you

you were flaxen-haired,
undernourished, and your
tar-black face was beautiful.
My poor scapegoat,

I almost love you
but would have cast, I know,
the stones of silence.
I am the artful voyeur

of your brain's exposed
and darkened combs,
your muscles' webbing
and all your numbered bones:

I who have stood dumb
when your betraying sisters,
cauled in tar,
wept by the railings,

who would connive
in civilized outrage
yet understand the exact
and tribal, intimate revenge.

her shaved head
like a stubble
of black corn,
her blindfold a soiled
bandage

The Guttural Muse

Late summer, and at midnight
I smelt the heat of the day:
At my window over the hotel car park
I breathed the muddied night airs off the lake
And watched a young crowd leave the discothèque.

Their voices rose up thick and comforting
As oily bubbles the feeding tench sent up
That evening at dusk – the slimy tench
Once called the 'doctor fish' because his slime
Was said to heal the wounds of fish that touched it.

A girl in a white dress
Was being courted out among the cars:
As her voice swarmed and puddled into laughs
I felt like some old pike all badged with sores
Wanting to swim in touch with soft-mouthed life.

I felt like some old pike all
badged with sores

The Haw Lantern

The wintry haw is burning out of season,
crab of the thorn, a small light for small people,
wanting no more from them but that they keep
the wick of self-respect from dying out,
not having to blind them with illumination.

But sometimes when your breath plumes in the frost
it takes the roaming shape of Diogenes
with his lantern, seeking one just man;
so you end up scrutinized from behind the haw
he holds up at eye-level on its twig,
and you flinch before its bonded pith and stone,
its blood-prick that you wish would test and clear you,
its pecked-at ripeness that scans you, then moves on.

Eavan **Boland**

(b. 1944)

What We Lost

Love

Eavan Boland was born in Dublin. Her father was a senior diplomat: Irish ambassador during her childhood at the Court of St James and then to the United Nations. Her mother was a painter, trained in France, her work on view at the National Gallery. Her mother's foster-mother was a fine story-teller and into the young poet's childhood her mother introduced 'this wonderful fragrance of the unrational, the inexplicable, the eloquent fragment'. 'What We Lost' from the sequence 'Outside History' evokes the broken narratives between women. When the stories are forgotten the artefacts, the made and cherished things, are the only 'text' a woman has to work with in making connections, discovering the active verbs and running syntax of a sentence she can call her own.

She lived in London from six to 12, out of place on account of her accent and her culture. Then the family moved to New York. She returned to Ireland in her mid-teens to school. Before going up to university she took a job and saved to print her first pamphlet of poems in 1963. She attended Trinity College, Dublin. Apart from the intellectual stimulus of that environment, there were deprivations she began to feel. The 'genderless poem' is what was expected of her. There was the danger of becoming an honorary male poet. Resisting, she began to apprehend her Irishness and her womanhood as things given, positive and in the broadest sense political.

Boland attended the Iowa Writers' Workshop. Her first book, *New Territory*, appeared in 1967. She had already begun to break away physically and imaginatively from the Dublin scene, to create a gendered space and insist on its different boundaries and its very distinct dynamic. 'I went to the suburbs. I married. I had two children.' Here she discovered, as she wrote, 'that what went into the Irish poem and what stayed outside it was both tense and hazardous for an Irish woman poet.' Irish women have had to negotiate from being objects in the Irish poem to being authors of it. In earlier poems 'you could have a political murder but not a baby'. It was a time of adjustment. In 1975 *The War Horse* appeared, an uneasy collection, followed by two books which mark a radical departure for her. *In Her Own Image* (1980) and *Night Feed* (1982) contain poems which confront the subject-matter of love, womanhood and motherhood – the physiology, the tensions and emotions of the complex domestic vocation. It was a case of 'the visionary risk of the life I lived becoming the poems I wrote'. Boland was writing 'a whole psychic terrain' into the Irish poem for the first time.

Of her feminism she says it is 'an enabling perception but it's not an aesthetic one. The poem is a place – at least for me – where all kinds of certainties stop. All sorts of beliefs, convictions, certainties get left on that threshold. I couldn't be a feminist poet. Simply because the poem is a place of experience and not a place of convictions ...'

Boland understands what she is up to. Her major sequences often appear alongside a substantial essay, telling herself and her readers what she intends, discussing the difficulties of composition and defining the space the poem occupies. *Object Lessons*, her most substantial prose work, considers some of the things she has had to do and things she has had to exclude. The 2005 *New Collected Poems* reveals how rapidly a poet who takes risks one at a time can move, and how far she can go.

What We Lost

It is a winter afternoon.
The hills are frozen. Light is failing.
The distance is a crystal earshot.
A woman is mending linen in her kitchen.

She is a countrywoman.
Behind her cupboard doors she hangs sprigged,
stove-dried lavender in muslin.
Her letters and mementoes and memories

are packeted in satin at the back with
gaberdine and worsted and
the cambric she has made into bodices;
the good tobacco silk for Sunday Mass.

She is sewing in the kitchen.
The sugar-feel of flax is in her hands.
Dusk. And the candles brought in then.
One by one. And the quiet sweat of wax.

There is a child by her side.
The tea is poured, the stitching put down.
The child grows still, sensing something of importance.
The woman settles and begins her story.

Believe it, what we lost is here in this room
on this veiled evening.
The woman finishes. The story ends.
The child, who is my mother, gets up, moves away.

In the winter air, unheard, unshared,
the moment happens, hangs fire, leads nowhere.
The light will fail and the room darken,
the child fall asleep and the story be forgotten.

The fields are dark already.
The frail connections have been made and are broken.
The dumb-show of legend has become language,
is becoming silence and who will know that once

words were possibilities and disappointments,
were scented closets filled with love-letters
and memories and lavender hemmed into muslin,
stored in sachets, aired in bed linen;

and travelled silks and the tones of cotton
tautened into bodices, subtly shaped by breathing;
were the rooms of childhood with their griefless peace,
their hands and whispers, their candles weeping brightly?

> The light will
> fail and the
> room darken,
> the child fall
> asleep and the
> story be
> forgotten.

Love

Dark falls on this mid-western town
where we once lived when myths collided.
Dusk has hidden the bridge in the river
which slides and deepens
to become the water
the hero crossed on his way to hell.

Not far from here is our old apartment.
We had a kitchen and an Amish table.
We had a view. And we discovered there
love had the feather and muscle of wings
and had come to live with us,
a brother of fire and air.

We had two infant children one of whom
was touched by death in this town
and spared: and when the hero
was hailed by his comrades in hell
their mouths opened and their voices failed and
there is no knowing what they would have asked
about a life they had shared and lost.

I am your wife.
It was years ago.
Our child was healed. We love each other still.
Across our day-to-day and ordinary distances
we speak plainly. We hear each other clearly.

And yet I want to return to you
on the bridge of the Iowa river as you were,
with snow on the shoulders of your coat
and a car passing with its headlights on:

I see you as a hero in a text –
the image blazing and the edges gilded –
and I long to cry out the epic question
my dear companion:

Will we ever live so intensely again?
Will love come to us again and be
so formidable at rest it offered us ascension
even to look at him?

But the words are shadows and you cannot hear me.
You walk away and I cannot follow.

my dear
companion:
Will we ever
live so
intensely
again?

James
Fenton
(b. 1949)

Born in Lincoln, James Fenton's background was emphatically English: Church of England, Repton School and Magdalen College, Oxford to read psychology and philosophy. Even as an undergraduate, he was a precocious poet, in this as in other respects resembling his chosen master, W.H. Auden. He won the Newdigate Prize with an accomplished sonnet sequence plus haikus called *Our Western Furniture*, about the opening of Japan to the West. The poet followed his poem east, as it were, becoming first a theatre critic and then a journalist in Germany, in Vietnam (he was the last Western journalist to leave the country), Korea and the Philippines.

Fenton was from a very early age fascinated by poetic forms and experiments. He was enchanted by the work of Marianne Moore, he loved Wallace Stevens, for a spell almost to distraction, and John Ashbery, about whom he has blown cold and hot. But always Auden has been his touchstone. His first book, *Terminal Moraine* (1972), suggested in its title an Audenesque landscape and time-scale, geological rather than simply historical. The poems within this book have many different forms and tones. He was and remains one of the subtlest humourous poets of his time, from found poems to outright satire to simple social comedy.

He experiments not only within poems but with books – the idea of the book itself being flexible. His most amusing 'book' was *Manila Envelope*, published when he lived in the Philippines: an A4 envelope full of poems on cards, posters and fold outs. Some of his finest work, including *A German Requiem* (1981), appeared first in pamphlet form, the poem being complete in itself, not part of a series or sequence.

Though he was very much a figure of the left in his university days and into the early years of his journalistic career, he did not put his poems to use in a conventional way. He often explores themes which for another poet would yield suasive statements and conclusions, but for Fenton in his 'civic' as in his love poems there is a sense of discovery in the process itself. Readers who followed Fenton's journalism describing his time in Germany were perhaps surprised to find passages from the prose closely echoed in and adapted for the *Requiem* with its brilliant way of making sense out of withholding sense. How spare can eloquence be? How far can a poet build on inadvertency? Thomas Hardy's 'The Man He Killed' (p.8) takes the same risk, making a statement out of its opposite, as it were.

Fenton's experiments are singular: he has not returned to the repetitive, insistent prosody of the *Requiem* in his subsequent work. He has, however, undertaken other kinds of experiment, in devising ways of counter-pointing metrical and free verse, for example, of using rhyme unexpectedly, of developing narrative in darkly suggestive ways.

He has developed a specifically public voice for some of his later work which is thinner in texture and easier in theme than much that has come before, as if he wishes to *appeal* to his audience. He has undeniably been drawn into the public sphere, as Professor of Poetry at Oxford for a period, as a journalist explaining the mechanics of poetry to the readers of newspapers, and as a critic. The sense of audience he has developed appears to have slowed up his muse and made him solicitous for his readers.

A German Requiem

It is not what they built. It is what they knocked down.
It is not the houses. It is the spaces in between the houses.
It is not the streets that exist. It is the streets that no longer exist.
It is not your memories which haunt you.
It is not what you have written down.
It is what you have forgotten, what you must forget.
What you must go on forgetting all your life.
And with any luck oblivion should discover a ritual.
You will find out that you are not alone in the enterprise.
Yesterday the very furniture seemed to reproach you.
Today you take your place in the Widow's Shuttle.

*

The bus is waiting at the southern gate
To take you to the city of your ancestors
Which stands on the hill opposite, with gleaming pediments,
As vivid as this charming square, your home.
Are you shy? You should be. It is almost like a wedding,
The way you clasp your flowers and give a little tug at your veil. Oh,
The hideous bridesmaids, it is natural that you should resent them
Just a little, on this first day.
But that will pass, and the cemetery is not far.
Here comes the driver, flicking a toothpick into the gutter,
His tongue still searching between his teeth.
See, he has not noticed you. No one has noticed you.
It will pass, young lady, it will pass.

*

How comforting it is, once or twice a year,
To get together and forget the old times.
As on those special days, ladies and gentlemen,
When the boiled shirts gather at the graveside
And a leering waistcoast approaches the rostrum.
It is like a solemn pact between the survivors.
They mayor has signed it on behalf of the freemasonry.
The priest has sealed it on behalf of all the rest.
Nothing more need be said, and it is better that way –

*

The better for the widow, that she should not live in fear of surprise,
The better for the young man, that he should move at liberty between the armchairs,
The better that these bent figures who flutter among the graves
Tending the nightlights and replacing the chrysanthemums
Are not ghosts,
That they shall go home.
The bus is waiting, and on the upper terraces
The workmen are dismantling the houses of the dead.

*

But when so many had died, so many and at such speed,
There were no cities waiting for the victims.
They unscrewed the name-plates from the shattered doorways
And carried them away with the coffins.
So the squares and parks were filled with the eloquence of young cemeteries:
The smell of fresh earth, the improvised crosses
And all the impossible directions in brass and enamel.

*

'Doctor Gliedschirm, skin specialist, surgeries 14–16 hours or by appointment.'
Professor Sargnagel was buried with four degrees, two associate memberships
And instructions to tradesmen to use the back entrance.
Your uncle's grave informed you that he lived in the third floor, left.
You were asked please to ring, and he would come down in the lift
To which one needed a key...

*

Would come down, would ever come down
With a smile like thin gruel, and never too much to say.
How he shrank through the years.
How you towered over him in the narrow cage.
How he shrinks now...

*

But come. Grief must have its term? Guilt too, then.
And it seems there is no limit to the resourcefulness of recollection.
So that a man might say and think:
When the world was at its darkest,
When the black wings passed over the rooftops
(And who can divine His purposes?) even then
There was always, always a fire in this hearth.
You see this cupboard? A priest-hole!
And in that lumber-room whole generations have been housed and fed.
Oh, if I were to begin, if I were to begin to tell you
The half, the quarter, a mere smattering of what we went through!

*

His wife nods, and a secret smile,
Like a breeze with enough strength to carry one dry leaf
Over two pavingstones, passes from chair to chair.
Even the enquirer is charmed.
He forgets to pursue the point.
It is not what he wants to know.
It is what he wants not to know.
It is not what they say.
It is what they do not say.

Glossary

Augustan In the eighteenth century in Britain a fascination with the Roman imperial age of Augustus contributed to a style of discourse which was classical, analytical, carefully proportioned and controlled.

Ballad A ballad was originally a form of popular poetry in an oral rather than a literary tradition, recounting heroic deeds. The literary ballad grew out of the popular ballad and imitated its directness and pace.

Cadence From the Latin word for 'fall', the word is used to describe the rhythmic pacing of language towards a resolution.

Concrete poetry This form of poetry, practised in Brazil and then in Scotland and elsewhere in Europe, treats the word form itself as an image and organizes type and lettering into spatial rather than sound structures on the page. (See Edwin Morgan's 'Siesta of a Hungarian Snake' (p147), which takes the fact that Hungarian is rich in s's and z's and makes play of this, using the convention of zzz to represent snoring.)

Elegy Originally a kind of reflective song, considering ephemerality, the word came to describe a poetic metre, and later on a poem of mood and atmosphere. Generally today it refers to a poem of mourning or regret.

Epiphany In the New Testament, Epiphany refers to the revelation of the Incarnation of Jesus to the wise men, the shepherds, and the world at large. It is used in secular terms (as, for example, in the writings of James Joyce, who makes much play of it) to refer to moments of sudden, clarifying insight.

Form 'Form' is hard to define in a modern literary work. Traditionally it referred to the prescribed structure a poet chose to work in: sonnet, ballad, couplet, blank verse etc. In Modernist and free form works it describes the progression between or balance of the constituent elements of sound, lineation, stanza break etc., those elements which organize and express the content of the poem.

Found poem A piece of language transposed from another context (an instruction manual, book of biology, history etc.), and without changing the actual words introducing poetic devices, in particular lineation, to make the same words in the same order express a sense in a different way.

Free verse Also known as unmetred verse, free verse rigorously avoids all predictable patterns of stress and all regularity of syllable count so that the reader must consider the rhythm of each line rather than follow a pre-established patterning.

Iambic pentameter The most commonly used English verse form, especially for verse drama (Marlowe, Shakespeare, Jonson etc.), the conventional iambic pentameter line consists of ten syllables divided into five 'feet', each of two syllables, the first of which is not accented (stressed), the second of which is.

Metaphysical In English poetry, the adjective 'metaphysical' attached to the poets of the late sixteenth and early seventeenth centuries (John Donne and George Herbert in particular) who developed elaborate metaphors, sometimes of considerable obscurity but generally of real fascination, in pursuit of effect (Donne) or religious truth (Herbert).

Metre The word comes from the Latin for 'measure' and describes any arrangement of language in which a regular number and pattern of accented syllables alternates with a regular number and pattern of unaccented syllables, making discrete 'feet', a 'foot' being a standard combination of accented and unaccented syllables. Trimeter, Tetrameter, Pentameter, Hexameter describe respectively verse lines with three, four, five and six feet.

Mimesis The Greek word for imitation, in poetry 'mimesis' is generally used to describe language which imitates or enacts, by sound or word order, the subject or image it is evoking.

Modernism In English poetry the term modernist is generally applied to the Anglo-American and Anglo-Irish writers who questioned poetic convention and redefined the tradition in terms which seemed to invalidate much that had come before. Artistic progressiveness was often matched by an aestheticization of politics which resulted in severe conservative or right-wing views. Ezra Pound, T.S. Eliot, James Joyce, W.B. Yeats and D.H. Lawrence are among the key figures in this very disparate movement.

New Criticism From the 1920s through to the mid 1960s, the new criticism held the ascendancy in schools and universities as the approved way of reading poetry. The key discipline was close reading of the texts and a deliberate exclusion from consideration of elements from outside the text, including biography. What the author intended was of less importance than what the poem intended and achieved. The particularism of the new critics remains a tonic, though the rigid exclusion of material useful for interpretation proved impoverishing.

Octosyllabic couplets A verse form in which each line has eight syllables and the lines are rhymed in pairs, aabbcc, as is the case with all couplets.

Prosody This describes the sound organization of a poem. It can be metrical (see 'metre' above), accentual (a repeating pattern of stressed syllables line by line), syllabic (a repeating syllable count line by line) or unmetred (a deliberate avoidance of regular patterning), or it can combine elements from two or more of these.

Quatrain A stanza (q.v.) of four lines.

Slant rhyme Exact rhyme is when the rhyming syllables have identical vowel and consonant values, e.g. mouse/house or juncture/puncture. In slant rhyme, the vowel values generally, but sometimes the consonant as well, are not identical, as in suck/book or stifle/ruffle.

Sonnet A poem of 14 iambic pentameter lines, usually rhyming. Sometimes the sonnet is divided into an octave (eight lines) and a sestet (six lines) with a change of emphasis or the beginning of the resolution of a syllogism occurring at the start of the sestet. Sometimes the sonnet is divided into three quatrains (q.v.) and resolves in a pentameter couplet.

Stanza This is a repeated grouping of lines in a poem. The shortest stanza is two lines (a couplet). Poems in which the divisions are irregular (e.g. a ten line section followed by a six, then a three) are not stanzaic, and it is better in such cases to speak of 'verse paragraphs'.

Stress In language, some syllables are spoken with more emphasis than others. EMPHasis, SPOken, SYLlables, LANguage. The emphasized syllables are said to be stressed, the unemphasized syllables are said to be unstressed, and metre consists in the regular patterning of stressed and unstressed syllables, and then in the playing of variations on the pattern.

Syllabic Syllables are the resolved units of sound out of which words are made. If we were to write a sentence with the syllables divided, it would look like this: Four score and se ven years a go, our fore fath ers brought forth on this con ti nent a new na tion. In syllabic poetry, there is a variable number of stresses (q.v.) but a regular number of syllables line by line. Syllabic verse is hard to write because the regularity it enforces is not readily audible; indeed good syllabic verse is proof against regularity of stress.

Syntax This term is used to describe the rules (nowadays construed descriptively rather than prescriptively) that determine how words as parts of speech (nouns, verbs, adjectives, adverbs, prepositions, conjunctions etc.) in or outside sentences combine in clauses and larger groupings to make meaning.

The Apocalyptics These poets were associated with the anthology *The New Apocalypse* (1939), edited by J.F. Hendry and Henry Treece, and characterized (the Second World War was beginning) by a sense of violent conjunctions and disjunctions in language. In the wake of the argumentative order of the generation of W.H. Auden, their poetry began beyond the containments of reason. Strangely enough, apart from the Surrealists, one of the chief influences on the work of some of them was the luminous and limpid poetry of Wallace Stevens. Two later anthologies appeared, *The White Horseman* (1941) and *Crown and Sickle* (1944).

The Beats Refers initially, in poetry, to the work of Allen Ginsberg whose *Howl* was its first substantial manifestation. His association with Jack Kerouac and William Burroughs is at the heart of it. Kerouac is said to have used the phrase first, some time in the late 1940s, to mean 'exhausted' or 'defeated', but Kerouac and Ginsberg insisted that it also implied upbeat and beatific and – in poetic terms – 'the beat' of the language.

The Black Mountain Poets Poets associated with Black Mountain College in Asheville, North Carolina, founded in 1933. Though the experiment lasted only just over two decades, it left a mark on all the arts, on education and philosophy. Buckminster Fuller, Merce Cunningham and John Cage are associated with it, and among poets Charles Olson (a professor and a key figure). Allen Ginsberg brought its influence to bear on the Beats.

The Fugitives A group of mainly southern US poets, most notably Allen Tate and John Crowe Ransom, who rejected the modernist approach to poetry and followed a radical, agrarian ideology. They published a magazine, *The Fugitive*, and *Fugitives: An Anthology of Verse*.

The Harlem Renaissance This term was applied to the great cultural flowering, centred in Harlem, New York City, and concentrated in the African-American community, which began around 1920 and lasted for more than a decade, through the Great Depression. Black writers found their way into the American mainstream in significant numbers for the first time, and their legacy proved durable.

The Imagists In the second decade of the century, this group centred in London around Ezra Pound and were openly hostile to the poetic conventions and establishment of the day. The first substantial Anglophone literary movement of the century, they espoused precision in language, an avoidance of abstraction, of moralizing, of narrative, and a bringing into focus of 'the image', not as an object in itself but as a point of fusion between perceptions. Pound made sure their work was grouped and published in magazines and crucially in four Imagist anthologies produced during the First World War (1914-1917). Eliot declared: 'The *point de repère* usually and conveniently taken as the starting-point of modern poetry is the group denominated "imagists" in London about 1910.'

The Movement was a drab term used by the editor of *The Spectator* in 1954 to describe a group of young writers (Kingsley Amis, Davie, Gunn, Larkin and others) who were specifically English, post-War and in articulate revolt against the excessive romanticism of the Apocalyptics (q.v.), their irrationality and deliberate avoidance of statement. There was an almost classical impulse in the movement, a sense of poetry as necessarily a responsible act, an art with a defined but limited social function.

The New York Poets Poets close to the visual arts and, largely through Frank O'Hara, associated with the New York School of painters, have come to be referred to as the New York Poets, the first generation of whom included, in particular, John Ashbery, Barbara Guest, Kenneth Koch, Frank O'Hara and James Schuyler.

The Objectivists The poets associated with Objectivism were second generation modernists who sought their paternity not in Eliot but in William Carlos Williams and felt a close affinity with the United States and a scepticism of the European legacy, except as mediated through Ezra Pound. Louis Zukofsky declared that the objectivist programme entailed acknowledging that a poem is an object, and that we should seek in it intelligence, sincerity, and a clarity of outlook, an effacement of subjectivity. Poets in the group included Williams, Zukofsky, George Oppen, Charles Reznikoff, and one Englishman, Basil Bunting.

The Vorticists Ezra Pound gave this brief movement its name and contributed to BLAST, the monumental journal that conveyed the literary and visual evidence of the group to a not much wider readership.

SOURCES & ACKNOWLEDGEMENTS

JOHN ASHBERY: 'What is Poetry', 'For John Clare', 'At North Farm', 'Just Walking Around', 'Annuals and Perennials', 'Some Trees' and 'What is Written', from Selected Poems (Carcanet Press, 1998), reprinted by permission of the publisher.

W.H.AUDEN: 'Twelve Songs. IX', 'Lullaby', 'Musée des Beaux Arts' and 'The Shield of Achilles' from Collected Shorter Poems 1927–1957 (Faber & Faber, 1969).

JAMES K. BAXTER: 'Morning and Evening Calm', from Jerusalem Sonnets, Sonnet 36, 'Haera Ra', 'Moss on plum branches' and 'A Pair of Sandals' from The Collected Poems of James K. Baxter (Oxford University Press, 2004).

JOHN BETJEMAN: 'The Plantster's Vision', 'A Shropshire Lad', 'The Licorice Fields at Pontefract' and 'The Last Laugh' from Collected Poems (John Murray, 1979), reprinted by permission of the publisher.

ELIZABETH BISHOP: 'Over 2000 Illustrations and a Complete Concordance' from The Complete Poems 1927–1979 (Farrar, Straus & Giroux, 1983), © 1979, 1983 by Alice Helen Methfessel.

EAVAN BOLAND: 'What We Lost' and 'Love' from Collected Poems (Carcanet Press, 1995), reprinted by permission of the publisher.

KAMAU BRATHWAITE: 'Calypso. I', from 'Islands and Exiles' in The Arrivants: A New World Trilogy (Oxford University Press, 1973).

BASIL BUNTING: from 'Chomei at Toyama (1932)' from Complete Poems (Bloodaxe Books, 2000).

E. E. CUMMINGS: 'in Just-', 'what if a much of a which of a wind' and 'pity this busy monster, manunkind' from Complete Poems 1904–1962, edited by George J. Firmage (Liveright, 1994), © 1991 by the Trustees for the E. E. Cummings Trust and George J. Firmage, reprinted by permission of W. W. Norton & Company.

DONALD DAVIE: 'Time Passing, Beloved', 'Aubade', 'Portland' and 'Their Rectitude Their Beauty' from Collected Poems (Carcanet Press, 1990), reprinted by permission of the publisher.

KEITH DOUGLAS: 'Cairo Jag', 'Vergissmeinnicht' and 'How to Kill' from The Complete Poems (Faber & Faber, 2004).

T. S. ELIOT: 'La Figlia Che Piange' and 'The Love Song of J. Alfred Prufrock' from Collected Poems 1909–1962 (Faber & Faber, 1974), reprinted by permission of Harcourt Inc.

JAMES FENTON: 'A German Requiem' from The Memory of War and Children in Exile: Poems 1968–1983 (Penguin Books, 1983), © James Fenton, reprinted by permission of PFD on behalf of James Fenton.

ROBERT FROST: 'The Runaway', 'Mending Wall', 'Stopping by Woods on a Snowy Evening', 'Mowing', 'Out, Out', and 'The Road Not Taken' from The Poetry of Robert Frost, edited by Edward Connery Lathem (Jonathan Cape, 1969), reprinted by permission of The Random House Group Ltd.

ALLEN GINSBERG: 'Kaddish. I' from Selected Poems 1947–1995 (Penguin Twentieth-Century Classics, 1997), reprinted by permission of Penguin Books Ltd.

W. S. GRAHAM: 'Gigha', 'Imagine a Forest' and 'I Leave This At Your Ear For When You Wake...' from New Collected Poems (Faber & Faber, 2004), © Michael and Margaret Snow, reprinted by permission of Michael Snow.

ROBERT GRAVES: 'The Cool Web', 'In Broken Images' and 'To Juan at the Winter Solstice' from Complete Poems In One Volume, edited by Patrick

Quinn (Carcanet Press, 2000), reprinted by permission of the publisher.

THOM GUNN: 'My Sad Captains' and 'Touch' from Collected Poems (Faber & Faber, 1993), and 'The Hug' from The Man with Night Sweats (Faber & Faber, 1992).

SEAMUS HEANEY: 'Punishment', 'The Gutteral Muse' and 'The Haw Lantern' from New Selected Poems 1966–1987 (Faber & Faber, 1990).

GEOFFREY HILL: 'Genesis' from For the Unfallen (1959), 'September Song' and 'Ovid in the Third Reich from King Log (1968), in Collected Poems (Penguin International Poets, 1985), reprinted by permission of Penguin Books Ltd.

A. E. HOUSMAN: 'Reveille', 'On Wenlock Edge, the wood's in trouble', 'Into my heart an air that kills' and 'Crossing alone the nighted ferry' from Collected Poems and Selected Prose (Penguin Twentieth-Century Classics, 1989), reprinted by permission of The Society of Authors as the Literary Representative of the Estate of A. E. Housman.

LANGSTON HUGHES: 'The Negro Speaks of Rivers', 'My People', 'Cross' and 'I Too' from Collected Poems of Langston Hughes (Alfred A. Knopf, 1994), reprinted by permission of David Higham Associates.

TED HUGHES: 'Wodwo', 'God Help the Wolf After Whom The Dogs Do Not Bark' and stanza II from 'Two Legends' from Collected Poems of Ted Hughes (Faber & Faber, 2005).

LAURA (RIDING) JACKSON: 'A City Seems' from First Awakenings: the early poems of Laura Riding, by Laura (Riding) Jackson, copyright © 1992, 'The Troubles of a Book' and 'The World and I' from The Poems of Laura Riding by Laura (Riding) Jackson, copyright © 1938, 1980, 2001, reprinted by permission of Carcanet Press, Manchester, Persea Books, New York, and the Laura (Riding) Jackson Board of Literary Management.

[In conformity with the wishes of the late Laura (Riding) Jackson, her Board of Literary Management asks us to record that, in 1941, Laura (Riding) Jackson renounced, on grounds of linguistic principle, the writing of poetry: she had come to hold that "poetry obstructs general attainment to something better in our linguistic way-of-life than we have".]

ROBINSON JEFFERS: 'Shine Perishing Republic', 'Return', 'Fire on the Hills' and 'The Stars Go Over the Lonely Ocean' from Selected Poems (Carcanet Press, 1987), reprinted by permission of the publisher.

THOMAS KINSELLA: 'Soft, To Your Places', 'The Laundress' and 'A Portrait of the Artist' from Collected Poems (Carcanet Press, 2001), reprinted by permission of the publisher.

RUDYARD KIPLING: 'Mesopotamia 1917', 'My Boy Jack' and 'The Storm Cone' from Selected Poems, edited by Peter Keating (Penguin Twentieth-Century Classics, 1993).

PHILIP LARKIN: 'Deceptions', 'Ambulances', 'MCMXIV' and 'The Trees' from Collected Poems (Faber & Faber, 1990), © the Estate of Philip Larkin, 1988.

D. H. LAWRENCE: 'Snake' from The Complete Poems of D. H. Lawrence by D. H. Lawrence, edited by V. de Sola Pinto and F. W. Roberts, copyright © 1964, 1971 by Angelo Ravagli and C. M. Weekly, Executors of the Estate of Frieda Lawrence Ravagli, reprinted by permission of Viking Penguin, a division of Penguin Group (USA) Inc.

ROBERT LOWELL: 'Home After Three Months Away', 'For The Union Dead' and 'Epilogue' from Collected Poems (Farrar, Straus & Giroux, 2000).

HUGH MACDIARMID: 'The Innumerable Christ', 'At My Father's Grave', 'Light and Shadow' and 'Crystals Like Blood' from Selected Poems (Penguin Twentieth-Century Classics, 1994), reprinted by permission of Carcanet Press.

CHARLOTTE MEW: 'Fame', 'Not For That City', 'Sea Love', 'Rooms' and 'The Peddler' from Collected Poems and Prose edited by Val Warner (Virago/Carcanet Press, 1982), reprinted by permission of Carcanet Press.

EDNA ST. VINCENT MILLAY: 'Time does not bring relief; you all have lied', 'Recuerdo', 'Wild Swan' and

'The Fawn' from Collected Poems (Harper & Row, 1956).

MARIANNE MOORE: 'To a Snail', 'What Are Years?' and 'The Mind is an Enchanting Thing' from Complete Poems (Faber & Faber, 1984).

EDWIN MORGAN: 'Siesta of a Hungarian Snake', 'A View of Things', 'Columba's Song' and 'Sir James Murray' from Collected Poems (Carcanet Press, 1990), reprinted by permission of the publisher.

LES MURRAY: 'An Absolutely Ordinary Rainbow', 'Cockspur Bush' and 'The Meaning of Existence' from Collected Poems (Carcanet Press, 1995), reprinted by permission of the publisher.

FRANK O'HARA: 'Autobiographia Literaria', 'Why I am not a Painter' and 'The Day Lady Died' from Selected Poems (Carcanet Press, 1998), reprinted by permission of the publisher.

SYLVIA PLATH: 'Daddy' from Collected Poems (Faber & Faber, 1981).

EZRA POUND: 'Speech for Psyche in the Golden Book of Apuleius' from Personae. The Shorter Poems of Ezra Pound (New Directions, 1990), and 'The River Merchant's Wife: A Letter', from Hugh Selwyn Mauberley. IV & V and from Canto LXXXI in Selected Poems 1908–1969 (Faber & Faber, 1977).

ADRIENNE RICH: 'The Burning of Paper instead of Children' from The Will to Change: Poems 1968–1970 (W. W. Norton, 1971).

C. H. SISSON: 'The Usk' and 'Anchises' from Collected Poems (Carcanet Press, 1998), reprinted by permission of the publisher.

WALLACE STEVENS: 'The Idea of Order at Key West', 'The Emperor of Ice-Cream', 'Thirteen Ways of Looking at a Blackbird', 'The Snow Man' and 'Final Soliloquy of the Interior Paramour' from Selected Poems (Faber & Faber, 1986).

ALLEN TATE: 'Ode to the Confederate Dead' from Collected Poems (Farrar, Straus & Giroux, 1977).

DYLAN THOMAS: 'The Force That Through The Green Fuse Drives The Flower', 'The Hand That Signed The Paper', 'A Refusal To Mourn, The Death By Fire, Of A Child In London' and 'Do Not Go Gentle Into That Good Night' from Collected Poems 1934–1952 (J. M. Dent, 1977).

DEREK WALCOTT: 'Adios, Carenage' from 'The Schooner Flight' in The Star-Apple Kingdom (Jonathan Cape, 1979).

WILLIAM CARLOS WILLIAMS: 'The Red Wheelbarrow', 'This is Just to Say', 'The Hunters in the Snow', 'Landscape with the Fall of Icarus' and 'The Great Figure' from Collected Poems (Carcanet Press, 2000), reprinted by permission of the publisher.

W. B. YEATS: 'An Irish Airman Foresees His Death', 'Easter 1916', 'The Second Coming', 'Sailing to Byzantium' © 1928 by The Macmillan Company; copyright renewed © 1956 by Georgie Yeats, 'Leda and the Swan' © 1928 by The Macmillan Company; copyright renewed © 1956 by Georgie Yeats and 'Long-legged Fly' © 1940 by Georgie Yeats; copyright renewed © 1968 by Bertha Georgie Yeats, Michael Butler Yeats and Anne Yeats from Collected Poems (Picador, 1990), reprinted by permission of A.P. Watt Ltd on behalf of Michael B. Yeats, and Scribner, an imprint of Simon & Schuster Adult Publishing Group

PICTURE CREDITS: Corbis, pp 6, 10, 14, 18, 28, 34, 38, 44, 48, 52, 58, 62, 66, 72, 76, 84, 88, 92, 104, 112, 118, 126, 130, 160, 178, 182, 194, 202, 218; Christopher Barker, pp 96, 108, 122, 136, 144, 148, 152, 190, 198, 210; Getty Images: pp 164, 168; Vanderbilt University Archives p100; Alexander Turnbull Library p156; p186 Paul Beasley/57 Productions